A General Speaks

Attention Authors

Manas Publications is fighting a war to tell the world that India can win the battle not only by bullet but also by pen. We are converting fighters into writers since our country is full of intellectuals but their knowledge is only confined to them. No sincere effort has been made by any publisher to give the right direction to their knowledge and the talent of intellectual is still hidden. An author always gives the raw material in the shape of manuscript and it is the sense of publisher to make it a finished product. We are motivating the intellectuals' mind and publishing their manuscripts for more than two decades and would like to publish your manuscript too. If you or your colleagues have any manuscript or are working on, please don't hesitate to contact us with detailed synopsis and contents for its publication. We take utmost care in production and give a wide publicity to the book and its author. We can also suggest you the title for writing related to your subject, since we are the publishers who believe more in quality than in quantity.

A General Speaks

General S. Padmanabhan (Retd.)
PVSM, AVSM, VSM
Former Chief of the Army Staff, India

Manas Publications
New Delhi-110 002 (INDIA)

MANAS PUBLICATIONS
(We Convert Fighters into Writers)
(Publishers, Distributors, Importers & Exporters)
4402/5-A, Ansari Road (Opp. HDFC Bank)
Darya Ganj, New Delhi-110 002 (INDIA)
Off. ☎ 23260783, 23265523, Res. 23842660
Fax: 011-23272766
E-mail: manaspublications@gmail.com
manaspublications@yahoo.com
website: www.manaspublications.in

2nd Impression 2014 (FP - 2005)

ISBN: 13 Digits - 978-81-7049-249-8
10 Digits - 81-7049-249-1

₹ 495/-

Designed at
Manas Publications

Printed in India at
HS Offsets, Delhi and published by Mrs Suman Lata for
Manas Publications, 4402/5-A, Ansari Road,
(Opp. HDFC Bank),
Darya Ganj, New Delhi-110 002 (INDIA)

Dedication

This book is dedicated to the 'Jawan', India's Soldier, as a token of my appreciation of his Courage, Loyalty, Steadfastness and Patriotism.

Acknowledgements

An anthology of essays on a variety of subjects entails even greater amount of research than a 'single subject' book. I found myself constantly needing assistance in the form of books, papers, CDs and floppies on a variety of subjects and am most grateful to Lt Gen Richard Khare and Lt Gen Deepak Summanwar who met all my demands with promptness and unfailing courtesy.

I would like to thank Maj Gen Paramjit Singh and Col Jason Peter for making available to me the resources of the Area H.Q. Library and in meeting some of my 'outsourced' research requirements. Without their help, writing this book would have been an uphill task.

I must also thank Mr. R Chandrashekar of Army H.Q. and Brig S. Dangwal of ASPT for their valuable contribution regarding sports in India.

I acknowledge with deep gratitude the help given to me by Messrs Christopher, Jayanathan and Balbir, all serving today in the Indian Army, for giving me detailed accounts of their recruitment and training. 'India's Soldier' is richer for their help.

My wife Roopa and daughter Lakshmi assisted me with very useful research work and acted as sounding boards for my ideas on numerous occasions. My special thanks to them.

I am also very grateful to G. Ashok Kumar for his excellent secretarial support and complete involvement in the writing of this book.

I must specially thank my old friend and fellow Rimcollian (name withheld as desired by him) for carefully going through the manuscript and making so many useful suggestions.

Finally, I must thank Mr. Vivek Garg of Manas Publications for his encouragement to write this book and patience in waiting a long time for it.

Preface

During my long military career of 43 years, I went through many experiences, met many people and faced numerous situations, ranging from the commonplace to the extraordinary. Ever since I retired, my friends have been urging me to write my 'Memoirs', or, at least about my military career. Such well-meant suggestions placed me in a quandary as my military career spanned across two thirds of my life! What should I put in and what should I leave out of this book? It certainly was a problem.

After considerable thought, I decided to write on various topics which I judged were topical, of interest to both military and non-military readers and which could be of some service to our country. This anthology of essays is the result.

The views I hold on many issues are quite different from those of the Government of India and of a number of my friends. I have stated these in unambiguous language in the essays. I have also taken a studied position on certain national security and foreign policy issues. These are my personal views and neither the Government nor Army Headquarters have anything to do with these. I alone am responsible for them.

I am conscious of a certain disjointedness about the book as a whole. This is inevitable in any anthology. However, to those who seek continuity in all that they read, I am happy to suggest that each chapter is thematically designed to contribute to the growth and betterment of our country, India. So I offer you this book for happy reading and serious contemplation about India and her future.

S Padmanabhan

Contents

1

The New Millennium Army

Human beings and conflict appear to be inextricably linked. From times immemorial, man has fought fellow man for a variety of reasons and sometimes, for no reason at all. Perhaps, all this fighting is part of the process of 'natural selection' in which only the fittest survives. At the dawn of history, human family units got organized into clans. Villages and larger social groupings like towns, cities and countries evolved over a period of time. People began to specialize in one occupation or the other such as farming, commerce, teaching, fighting and so on. The specialists in fighting were the progenitors of armies, the symbol of power of a modern nation and the guardians of its frontiers.

The Indian Army too, has evolved over the millennia: from being the army of a tribe to be that of Porus; from being the army of Shivaji to be that of the Moghuls and the British; to becoming the army of Independent India on 15th August 1947. This evolution went on, while important developments were taking place elsewhere in the world. The taming of the horse and invention of the stirrup, the development of firearms, the advent of machines of the Industrial Age, the birth of the Bomb and now the dawn of the Information Age – these are a few of such developments, each of which has caused a revolution in military affairs and shaped the course of evolution of the armies, the world over. The Indian Army too is a product of this ongoing process. Let us see how our Army had evolved by the end of the 20th century.

As a nation, we had missed the Industrial Revolution. We became a colony of the British. Our Army took shape under the British and some of our Rajas and Maharajas, into a tough, professional force, well led but ill equipped, potentially lethal but chronically too poor to realise its full potential. We paid the price for this neglect during the colonial and the post independence era when we suffered a humiliating defeat at the hands of the Chinese in 1962. But we bounced back from the depths of this defeat to the pinnacle of success in 1971, when, after a brief war against Pakistan, we emerged as the unquestioned victors. Some years later, we went overseas to the aid of the Maldives and Sri Lanka. The latter experience brought home to us the important lesson that good intentions and valour alone will not suffice; prudence and discretion too are essential for success.

In 1999, the Kargil experience made us invest heavily in 'force multipliers' for, without these, the effectiveness of armies cannot really be maximised. Modern technology must supplement the undoubted fighting skill of the Indian soldier. So, the picture of Indian Army at the dawn of the Third Millennium is of a large, million-plus strong army, battle tested, sound at heart, but beset by problems of low availability of modern technology, fairly high levels of obsolescence of weapons, equipment and electronics and not yet being benefited by the advent of the Information Age in any significant manner.

This then is the Indian Army that bravely faces the challenges of the 21st century.

Let us examine the geo-strategic scenario which lies ahead in the first 25 years of the 21st century. We shall first look at the world scenario in general terms and thereafter the regional and national scenarios in relation to one another.

The world became unipolar after the demise of the Soviet Union. It continues to be so with the USA being the unchallenged superpower. This situation seems likely to continue for another 15 to 20 years by which time, the world order may change to a multipolar configuration with China, Europe and possibly Japan becoming important power centres by virtue of their economic power or military power, or both. We see the process of globalisation of the economy well underway. The increasing interdependence of nations on one another for technology and resources and the general onset of the Information Age will combine to make it impossible for any country to insulate itself from others. Thus, whether a nation wishes to or not, it has to be a world level player and within the bounds of the prevailing world order, it has to seek its strategic space.

Asia is a rapidly developing region. China, India, Japan, the ASEAN countries, the Koreas, the oil-rich lands of West Asia and the small but gas and oil-rich Central Asian republics, all lie in this region. China seeks to achieve 'great power' status by around 2015 and 'superpower' status by 2025-2030. Japan, the 'Asian Tigers' and some of the West Asian countries have achieved considerable economic stability either through spectacular use of science and technology or by using their natural resources (mainly oil) to garner economic wealth for their people. Sadly, the countries like India and Pakistan, North Korea and South Korea, Iran and Iraq have continued their hostile relations of the last century and been depriving themselves of the opportunity for unhindered progress.

There is also a new presence in Asia – the USA. After its war on Afghanistan, the USA has installed a regime in Kabul which it approves of. The USA now jealously guards its new client-state with its forces located both within Afghanistan and in nearby countries like Pakistan, Uzbekistan, Tajikistan and Kirghizstan. Again, having dealt with Iraq in a similar manner, the American forces and those of its allies are in occupation of that hapless country where, though President Bush proclaimed the 'end of the war' in May 2003, there is no peace. Pakistan too has a considerable American presence with the US military bases on its soil and a regime that is patronised by the USA and proclaimed by it to be a major non-NATO ally. Pakistan also receives monthly subventions of about $ 100 million for its logistic support to the US forces, a guarantee of $ 3 billion over five years and a 'write-off' of $ 450 million of debts. The regional strategic scenario, therefore, may be summed up as being heavily dominated by the USA in West Asia, parts of Central Asia and Pakistan; and by China in East Asia.

Three other matters deserve special mention before we turn away from the Asian region. The first is the advent of nuclear weapons in at least three countries – India, Israel and Pakistan. The second is a steady depletion of the region's oil reserves which may last till 2050 if husbanded prudently. And rather more disturbing than nuclear weapons or resource depletion is the rapid growth of non-state international terrorism which exploits religion to gain adherents to its cause (whatever it might be) and has succeeded in giving even the mighty USA an acute case of paranoia from which it has yet to recover. Overall, for a variety of reasons such as religious, ethnic and economic rivalries as well as the competition for dwindling natural resources, this region has become specially volatile and may remain so during the foreseeable future.

Let us now focus on India as we step into the 21st century. Even a brief look is enough to indicate that this nation of over one billion people has woken up after its two centuries of slumber under the British colonial rule and half a century of post-Independence experimentations with concepts such as 'command' economy. Well endowed by Nature in terms of high quality manpower and natural resources, we have the potential to become one of the giants of the world economy. We are already world leaders in IT software and our IT professionals are the most sought after people in the Western world. Now, with the privatisation of the economy, general restructuring and dismantling of the regime of quotas and permits, our economic health has improved and is likely to get better in the days to come.

A sustained rate of growth of over seven per cent per annum over the next decade or so appears entirely possible. Clearly, India's economy, which is the fourth largest in the world, is steadily progressing to be ranked as the largest economy in the decades ahead.

Lest we should deceive ourselves by the tales that statistics tell, let us also face some ugly truths. Large sections of India's vast population live below the poverty line. They are under-nourished, lack the very necessities of life such as food, clothing, shelter, safe drinking water and electricity. They are poorly accessed by roads and are often incapable of reaching medical help in times of acute emergencies. This is the 'other India' where poverty, hunger, disease and despair still prevail; where rain-dependent farmers frequently commit suicide as they are unable to bear the heavy debts they incurred in the lean years. In this 'other India', people do not care for GDP related growth rates or intellectual property rights. They ask only for the right to live, to work and the basic dignity of life desired by any human being.

We must also take note of certain serious 'drag' factors which sap the vitality of this great nation and prevent it from realising its full potential. Tardiness in completing the process of nation building and distorting or even destroying democratic institutions created by the founding fathers of free India – these have weakened much of our claim of being the largest, genuine democracy in the world. We are beset by separatist movements : problems like that of Jammu and Kashmir; problems originating in sub-nationalism in the north-eastern states; problems rooted in centuries of economic deprivation and injustice such as the Naxalite movement and its latter day derivatives; communal problems in many of the states; and gnawing at our vitals like a deep-rooted cancer, the problem of all-pervading corruption. Unless these clearly identifiable problems are faced and overcome, a glorious India will remain a mirage, no matter what our rate of growth might be. This really is the core issue for India as it bravely enters the new millennium: can we overcome the separatist movements, bring within the reach of every Indian family the necessities of life, eliminate corruption and grow at a sustained rate of over seven per cent while ensuring distributive justice among the people? If we can do all this while holding on to the values of integrity, probity, fellow-feeling, communal tolerance and compassion, we would indeed have created the greatest nation the world has ever seen.

It is this India that the Indian Army has been tasked to safeguard and defend. Let us focus on the role allotted to the Indian Army and take stock of how it is endowed to face the challenges of the new millennium.

The Indian Army, like most of the other armies of the world, is maintained by the country to safeguard its core values and national interests. Our Army, in addition to this traditional role, contributes to national integration and stability through its actions in times of natural or man-made disasters and by being an example to the people at large of true national unity. Analysis of the role of the Indian Army will reveal that it must possess a number of military capabilities so that it may fulfill the role allotted. What are these military capabilities? These are:

- *Deterrent Capability:* The Army should be strong enough in terms of conventional strength as well as in nuclear weapons to deter any potential aggressor.
- *War Fighting Capability:* In case deterrence fails, the Army should be able to operate effectively in both conventional as well as in nuclear-biological-chemical warfare situations.
- *Conflict Management Capability:* The Army should be able to deal with and manage internal conflict situations such as counter-insurgency operations, internal security operations and so on.
- *Force Projection Capability*: Under special circumstances, the Army should be able to send the land component of a joint task force for 'out of area' operations.
- *Peace Keeping Capability:* The Army should be able to fulfill UN peace keeping missions in any part of the world.

It is our assessment that the Indian Army, as it entered the 21st century, possessed all these capabilities to a substantial extent and had actually demonstrated these in actions, in the recent past. For example, after the 1971 defeat of Pakistan, they were effectively deterred from engaging us in conventional war because of our conventional force superiority. The Kargil fighting of 1999 did not escalate into a more general conventional war, mainly for two reasons – our somewhat diminished but nevertheless formidable conventional edge over Pakistan and the restraining influence of the USA and others on both the countries. The nuclear weapons capability of neither side was required though the fact that India had a 'survivable' second strike capability, would have served to cool any thought of a first strike by Pakistan despite its bellicose posturing. In relation to China, a superpower in the making, we possess adequate conventional deterrent capability but our nuclear forces do not give us the minimum deterrence against that country. In a situation where China and Pakistan are militarily allied against us, our conventional deterrent will be seriously strained and we would need external allies to steady our position. Whether or not our relations with China worsen to the extent of going for a war, is an issue by itself and will be considered elsewhere in this book. Suffice it to say that nations cannot rely only on the goodwill of other nations for their security. We must do what is necessary for our security.

In the management of internal conflicts, our Army has more experience than any other army in the world. What is more important is that the entire concept of internal conflict management has been rewritten by our Army. We learnt the hard way but what we learnt, we assimilated and applied in later situations. For instance, the concept of military-civic action is routinely practiced by our units in counter-insurgency operations. It was showcased by operations like 'Good Samaritan' in the states of Nagaland and Manipur and 'Sadhbhavana', first in Ladakh and later, elsewhere in Jammu and Kashmir. The importance of 'winning hearts and minds' as a principle of internal conflict management was well learnt by our Army. Everywhere, whenever our Army was called upon to manage internal security problems or a proxy war, it delivered results.

As to war fighting capability, 1971 saw the Indian Army fight a major war, the Indo-Pak War, and achieve victory. Since then, our Army was called upon to fight in the Siachen and Kargil sectors. In the Siachen sector, after 20 years of bitter fighting against the enemy and hostile environmental conditions, our forces still occupy all that we captured in 1984. And in Kargil, in 1999, our forces, though disadvantaged by initial reverses, covered themselves with glory unmatched anywhere in the annals of war. The war fighting capability of Indian Army may, therefore, be regarded as formidable in any terrain or climatic condition and in any form of warfare.

Our force projection capability within the region was demonstrated twice. The first occasion saw a parachute battalion group being airlifted to the Maldives at the request of the Maldivian government, who were apprehending a major threat from hostile mercenaries. The mission was executed in a professional manner, to the satisfaction of the Maldivian government and our forces returned home in a short period. The second occasion when our forces were deployed overseas, was in accordance with the Indo-Sri Lanka Agreement of 1987. As agreed, an Indian Peace Keeping Force (IPKF) was deployed in Sri Lanka with every hope that there would be no breach of the peace by any of the contending parties. But this did not happen and the IPKF was embroiled in active operations against the Liberation Tigers of Tamil Eelam. (LTTE). These operations were marked by intense violence and over 1100 Indian servicemen were killed in action. After two years, the IPKF was pulled back to India in response to a request from the Sri Lanka government of the time. Much was learned by the Indian Army from the IPKF experience. The vital requirement of accurate strategic and operational intelligence, the ability to switch from a peace keeping role per se to peace enforcement and the absolute importance of giving the army in the field full freedom to operate as demanded by the situation.

The Indian Army has an outstanding record in contributing forces and personnel for operations under the UN flag. Our role in support of the UN started in Korea and has continued without a break through various hot-spots in Asia, Africa and the Mediterranean. Our forces were sometimes required to fight while on an UN assignment, as in the Congo and later in Sierra Leone. The entire world acknowledged their magnificent performance in such operations. Even in very highly sensitised areas like Somalia where other national contingents had faced difficulty, the Indian soldier's humane and correct dealings won for him the desired result. By the turn of the last century, the Army had established a Centre for UN Peace Keeping Operations in New Delhi with the United Services Institution doing yeoman service for the cause. Not only are our personnel being trained there for UN assignments, we also receive regular requests from other countries to help train their personnel.

The five-fold capabilities which we must possess in order to fulfill our role as an army are, therefore, possessed in good measure by our Army. There are, no doubt, many areas where the desired level of capability eludes us – perhaps due to resource inadequacy or lack of clear policy decisions from the Government. In the next chapter we will examine how the Indian Army, well endowed and capable as we have just seen, fared in the first two years of the new millennium. We will attempt to focus on issues instead of personalities, as that is the best way to correct and improve ourselves where such actions are indicated.

2

The First Two Years: 2001 and 2002

I took over as Chief of the Army Staff (COAS) on 30th September, 2000. I was thoroughly familiar with the challenges being faced by our Army and those that lay ahead in the 21st century. It was clear to me that barring the unforeseen, our Army will have to defend our borders, fight the proxy war or insurgencies in some of our states, make good our manpower and material deficiencies and keep ourselves in readiness to fight a war or undertake UN missions. We had to do all this within the economic resources made available to us and in concert with the Navy and the Air Force. While doing all this, we had to ensure the upgradation of the military capabilities of our personnel and improve the quality of their lives in a comprehensive manner. All this sounds like a 'tall order'. However, this is exactly what every COAS normally faces when he takes over command of the Indian Army. The tasks ahead and my priorities for these were, therefore, clear to me on Day 1 of my command of this great Army. Let us see how we fared upto the end of 2002, when I handed over charge to my successor.

The 20th century ended with J&K and the North-East continuing to be in a state of unrest while counter-insurgency operations went on as before.

In J&K, the unilateral ceasefire against militants proclaimed on 19th November, 2000 (The Ramadan Ceasefire) was officially continuing though militants carried out systematic attacks against suspected 'informers' and their kinfolk and used the self-imposed restraint of the security forces in order to regroup and rebuild their strength. However, there was a condition of undeclared 'truce' on the Line of Control and the international border in the Jammu sector. Civilian and military casualties along the border areas, therefore, dropped significantly as did the Army's ammunition expenditure. In the interior however, both civilian and military casualties continued to occur and some militants too were neutralised in combats provoked by the militants. The Government, for its part, extended the ceasefire periodically till the third week of May 2001 when it decided to allow the 'ceasefire' to lapse – an acknowledgement of the existing ground realities, which were apparent even earlier.

During the ceasefire period, the Government nominated Mr KC Pant, the then Deputy Chairman of the Planning Commission (and a former Defence Minister), to hold talks with the militant groups and others in order to find ways to restore peace and normalcy in that troubled state. This well meant initiative failed to achieve any meaningful result. The reasons for this failure as well as the failure of the unilateral ceasefire or 'Non Initiation of Combat Operations (NICO)' as it was officially termed, were many. The core reason was that the controllers of terrorism in J&K—the Pakistani ISI, were not ready for it, yet.

The ceasefire in Nagaland and similar informal arrangements in Manipur continued with some hiccups. Former Home Secretary K Padmanabhiah was the official interlocutor in talks held with the NSCN (I-M) Group, the strongest group among the Naga insurgents. The talks continued despite numerous setbacks, and with each successive round of talks, there was a surge of hope that an agreement on the issues relating to Nagaland would be reached. This was specially so as the people of Nagaland had raised a sustained clamour for peace. Unfortunately, this was far from being the case in Manipur where violence continued and no solution to the problems besetting the state was in sight.

Assam was another area of concern with the ULFA and the Bodo activists indulging in periodic violence and causing much hardship to the people and the economy of the state. The Assam Accord of 1985 and the formation of the Bodoland Autonomous Council in 1993, provided a brief respite from its problems to the state. The internal security situation in the state at the turn of the century was far from peaceful. ULFA and Bodo militant camps were well established in Bhutan and hence immune to direct action by Indian forces. Within the state, periodic outbreaks of ethnic violence occurred, leading to much bloodshed. No section of the population was spared these bouts of blood-letting: Bodos, Santhals, Ahoms and migrants, the Reaper visited them with impartiality. The Army played a notable role in keeping the situation from exploding into a major conflagration and suffered some casualties in doing so. National assets, such as oil pipelines and commercial enterprises like tea gardens, were often interfered with while the forest wealth of the state was regularly looted. People went about their business, ever expecting a 'bandh' or demand for money – either as ransom for some abducted person or simply as a 'loyalty tax', paid to the militant group dominant in that area. Road traffic was similarly heavily mulcted, forcing transport vehicles to travel in convoys and only during day time. Assam, to all intents and purposes, was in a state of moderate to high unrest. There was, indeed, a Government at Dispur, Assam. However, it was difficult to identify very many areas where their writ ran except when backed up by the presence of the Army. It was a bad situation and even as we write these lines, it remains so.

The concluding days of the 20th century (22nd December, 2000) saw a bold terrorist action at the Red Fort, Delhi, apparently by a two or three-member suicide squad. They left two soldiers and a civilian dead and brought home to the people and the government the fact of their vulnerability to terrorist attacks. Though one of the persons involved in the attack was reported to have been killed on 26th December, the episode left no one in the Capital in any doubt about the safety of any place in India from terrorist attacks. Notwithstanding this new awareness, India's Parliament House was subjected to a 'suicide' attack by a terrorist squad on 13th December, 2001. Soon after, the Raghunath Temple in Jammu was attacked on 30th March, 2002 and the Swami Narayan Temple in Gandhinagar (Gujarat) on 24th September, 2002. There were numerous 'suicide' attacks in J&K during the period 2001-02. The abortive attack on Srinagar airport on 16th January, 2001, the killing of 13 pilgrims on their way to the holy Amarnath shrine on 21st July, 2001, the massacres on 4th August, 2001 in Kishtwar area in which 15 innocents were killed, the attacks at Jammu Railway Station in which 10 persons were killed, the 15th August, 2001 massacre of five persons in Mahore and the 4th November, 2001 killing of four persons at Petha Dyalgam, are incidents that readily come to mind. There were, of course, the grisly statistics generated by counter-insurgency operations in J&K in the course of which the terrorists suffered numerous casualties as did the security forces.

The picture that emerges at the end of 2002 is of India continuing with counter-insurgency operations, periodic peace initiatives and negotiating with the militant groups that were willing to talk but not really achieving anything that could be called a breakthrough. Militant groups though heavily mauled, even decimated, were able to continue in action, thanks to illicit support from Pakistan. Their ability to operate as in the past was, however, severely affected and this had reduced them to resort to rather luridly publicised suicide actions to retain their credibility among the people of J&K. In the process of doing so, they stepped over the threshold of tolerance of the Government of India when a suicide squad of five terrorists attacked India's Parliament House on 13th December, 2001, no doubt, with a view to decapitating India's top political leadership and killing or taking hostage our members of parliament. This led directly to a response from the Government against Pakistan which was clearly perceived as the source of this terrorist action, as indeed most of the terrorism afflicting India. The response culminated in Operation Parakram, the most massive deployment till date of the armed forces for war against our neighbour. But let us revert to the two years of my command and see what else transpired during 2001-2002 other than insurgencies and terrorism.

The first event that comes to mind is the tragic Gujarat earthquake which occurred on the morning of Republic Day, 2001. Measuring 6.9 on the Richter scale, this earthquake hit various parts of Gujarat at about 0830 hrs even as school children were assembling for Republic Day celebrations and large crowds thronged the streets and market places to participate in the festivity. Kutch was the worst affected. In all, the earthquake claimed over 2500 lives and property worth millions of Rupees was destroyed. A massive rescue and relief operation was launched with the Indian Army playing a major role. The Indian Air Force base at Bhuj was badly affected and many personnel lost their kith and kin. Despite this, Bhuj Air Force station functioned without any thought of personal grief and efficiently handled the huge quantities of international aid being flown in to Kutch. I thought that the quiet dedication and courage of the IAF personnel from Bhuj was magnificent. We owe much to them. The Indian Navy too played a very useful role in the management of casualties of the earthquake. Ships of the fleet did duty as floating hospitals and provided much needed support to the medical personnel operating on land – civilian and military, Indian and foreign.

A few words about the Disaster Relief Operations carried out by the Indian Army in Gujarat will not be out of place. Whether it was in the actions of the Gujarat based troops or those of the enginering, medical, logistic and combat units, moved in from elsewhere in the country, I noticed that the personnel were purposeful, motivated, determined and not baulked either by the enormity of the situation they faced or the paucity of specialised tools and equipment for their relief work. On 28th January, 2001, when I visited the field hospital set up by the Army at Bhuj under tarpaulin shelters, I met many a surgeon who had been on his feet, operating continuously for about 48 hours. Their dedication to duty and their spirit of 'service before self' made me feel proud as I shook hands with them and said 'thank you'. Their dedication had saved countless lives. I was also deeply touched by the tremendous fellow-feeling evinced by the average Indian. The poor and the rich, all sent aid for the disaster-hit people – from a set of aluminium vessels to millions of Rupees. I felt proud to be an Indian. In fact, the whole world helped handsomely. I understood what a 'global village' truly was.

The earthquake also brought home to me the fact that our Army was inadequately equipped to tackle the aftermath of such a disaster. Specialised plant and machinery, cutting tools, hoists of various types are just a few of these equipment. I was impressed by the Turkish team that had come in and were digging for survivors and dead bodies in the small town of Anchar. Clearly they had structured their unit on the basis of their past experiences with the earthquake that had devastated their country some time ago. They performed extremely well. The American team impressed us with the range of specialised equipment they had brought in. Having seen all this, on return to Delhi, I ordered a time-bound study to be carried out of Disaster Relief in general and the Army's role in it in particular. The study was duly done and the report was presented to the Ministry of Defence for acceptance and inter-ministerial action where required. Everyone was enthusiastic and added their refinements to it. Ultimately the report was buried under the sheer mass of papers generated by other departments/ministries and till date, no concrete action would appear to have been taken to better equip the Army for Disaster Relief. It is a great pity. I can only think of the Turkish detachment in Anchar and sadly shake my head at our ponderous, non-productive governmental machinery that does not respond with alacrity to the needs of the times. There is no sense in learning lessons but not acting on them. And yet, when the 'Tsunami' disaster struck southern India on 26th December, 2004, nobody who saw the Army in action had anything but praise for them. Perhaps we had leant something, after all!

After the tragic events of 26th January, 2001, the Army was hit by the 'Tehelka' revelations. Tehelka.com, in a 'sting' operation, exposed major weaknesses in the system of Defence procurements. It brought out the high degree of corruption that pervades Defence procurement procedures and the role of 'agents' or brokers for companies offering their products for sale to the Indian Army. It focused on political, bureaucratic and military corruption, the dubious role of ex-military officers acting for vendors and succeeded in trapping a number of persons through its 'sting' operation. I had to take action against some serving Army officers after due enquiry into the revelations of Tehelka.com about their actions. I must confess that action could not be completed till the end of 2002 in all cases due to legal hurdles and the efforts of many other persons involved in or interested in the case. Notwithstanding all these pulls and pressures, no case which had not been fully actioned has been closed. I understand, as we go to the press, that after four years, military justice finally has the guilty persons in its grip and they should hope to get their just deserts soon. While the Tehelka episode was indeed painful to all of us in the Army, it did achieve some positive results. Defence procurement procedures were revised and hopefully, improved. The then Minister for External Affairs, who was given additional charge of the Ministry of Defence, on the resignation of the incumbent following the Tehelka revelations, directed numerous studies to restructure the logistic services, including removing redundancies and streamlining their functioning. These were duly carried out and a number of changes for the better were brought about. Notwithstanding all this, the entire episode filled me with serious concern at the inroads made into public life by the evils of greed and corruption. I realised that as a 'slice' of the same public, the Army too, has been tainted to some extent by what I can only describe as India's Public Enemy Number One – Venality or Corruption. I resolved to do something about it in terms of strengthening our existing system of checks and balances, careful selection of officers to sensitive appointments and laying renewed emphasis on the Code of Ethics or the Honour Code.

One of my priority areas was training the Army for its operational tasks so that all formations were ready for combat at short notice. A number of exercises with troops were held at different levels and considerable attention was paid to joint training with the other two Services. Overall, I believe, we realised our training objectives to a very substantial extent.

Here, I must categorically state that neither are our training methods outdated nor are we training for 'the last war', as a senior journalist, who should have known better, once wrote. The problem with our civilian Defence experts is that they consider any foreign military doctrine, specially that of the USA, to be superior to ours. My advice to them would be to interact with the senior levels of the Army as well as attend exercises with troops to correlate concept and execution and the training that makes the execution possible. These senior journalists mean well and have deservedly high reputation. However, sweeping pronouncements on a subject they have little experience of, are bound to convey a wrong message to the soldiers and the civilians alike. The Army Training Command (ARTRAC) carries out detailed analysis of the future course of warfare as discerned from wide ranging research, study and observation of training methodology the world over, and evolves suitable doctrines to see that we train for wars of the present and future. I must add here that those who concentrate on either the past or the future to the exclusion of the present, are likely to suffer heavily.

Examples of this are legion: the Allied armies at the beginning of World War II illustrate how the 'Maginot Line' complex derived from past wars failed before the doctrine of 'Blitzkrieg' in which manoeuvre, firepower and joint land-air war were of the essence. And in today's context we can see how even the most modern of armies whose focus is on the future has, in the recent past, failed to achieve its aims before 'third world' armies such as Vietnam, and even Iraq in 2003-04. My belief is this: while it is necessary to look towards the future with one's head in the clouds, as it were, it is wise to have one's feet firmly planted on the ground. The current American plans for 'Force 21' with the concept of a 'transitional' Army bridging the 'present' and the 'objective' Army is wisely conceived. If this is backed by corresponding training doctrines, all will be well. If not, as in Iraq, a very well equipped Army will find itself struggling against irregular forces. I am satisfied that the Indian Army is training in a realistic and futuristic manner – for the 'here and now' and for the 'future', relating it to what our adversaries might become capable of by then. I confidently assert that regardless of what some persons say, our Army is training appropriately for war, now or later, with adversaries who are known or appreciated.

One of the positive outcomes of the post-Kargil 'soul-searching' was the decision to create the appointments of Chief of the Defence Staff (CDS) and his No. 2, the Vice Chief of the Defence Staff (VCDS). They were to be supported by an Integrated Defence Staff (IDS) headed by a Chief of Staff (COS). Unfortunately, this decision has been implemented only partially, as Government approval for creating the appointments of CDS and VCDS has not been given. We have, therefore, a situation where the Chief of Staff, Integrated Defence Staff, reports to the Chairman, Chiefs of Staff Committee

(COSC). It would appear that the Government has lost sight of the fact that the Chairman, COSC, is an appointment tenanted by the seniormost of the Service Chiefs and there will be many occasions when the incumbent may have a tenure of as little as one month! What kind of credibility the short-tenured Chairman's 'single point' advice to the Government on Defence matters will have, can be easily imagined. A Service Chief, today, can spend only a small part of his time on attending to matters under the purview of the COSC. His own service will necessarily demand his closest attention. He will, therefore, be over-dependent on the COS, IDS, on all joint-services matters. If, as could well happen, two successive Chairmen, COSC, hold office for only one month each, there is every possibility that the COS, IDS, will wield influence far in excess of what is justified by his rank (three star) and level of experience. This will bear directly on the quality of advice given to the Government by the Chairman, COSC. The gravity of this can be visualised in the event of war, specially in relation to matters pertaining to Strategic Forces Command, Andaman Nicobar Command, Defence Intelligence Agency and other integrated departments. I am convinced that the Government is wrong in not clearing the appointments of CDS and VCDS. The entire effort in creating an Integrated Defence Staff is, as of now, an exercise in futility as the organisation for which this staff has been created, is headless. In fact, without the CDS and VCDS, Integrated Defence Staff is yet another example of redundancy in military bureaucracy.

While on the subject of CDS, I have heard many (including senior, retired, service officers) refer to the CDS as if the appointment was to be treated as senior to that of the Service Chiefs. Some of them have talked of the CDS as being in overall command of the Armed

Forces and a few have even conferred 'five star' rank on the non-existent CDS! I am clear that the formulations of the Arun Singh Task Force (ASTF) which dealt with higher Defence organisations, did not visualise anyone with 'five star' rank and in fact, spoke of the CDS as 'first' among equals. 'Primus Inter Pares' suggests that CDS, like the Prime Minister, is to be treated as No. 1 among the Chiefs. Even this is not warranted because the CDS as conceived by ASTF has major 'managerial' functions as opposed to 'command' functions and even a newly promoted four star General/Flag/Air Officer could be appointed CDS. As such, CDS will be 'one' among the Chiefs and not their 'No.1'. But all this is academic. Where is the CDS? We have created a 'headless wonder' in the IDS. Will the Government now display the wisdom needed to provide the 'head' so that the organisation may realise the objects for which it was created? Or, will the Government take the advice of ill-informed persons and feel satisfied that they have blocked the rise of a potential military threat to India's democracy? Have they not learnt during the 58 years since India attained freedom that the Indian Armed Forces have been, are and will be, apolitical and thus have no 'praetorian' ambitions? It is time the Government reviewed its stand on the CDS and gave a decision without further delay.

The first two years of the 21st century also saw the two South Asian neighbours add to their nuclear arsenals and improve their delivery capability for nuclear weapons. Attempts to evolve their respective nuclear doctrines were undertaken with varying sense of urgency and speed. Pakistan had a very small decision loop as their President also doubled as the COAS, and while constitutional proprieties were seemingly observed, their decision making was essentially a one-man show, the President's. On the other hand, our process of decision making involved a great deal of consultation and discussion and though all this took longer time than our neighbour's, I believe our Strategic Weapons Doctrine is clear, unambiguous and complete.

On the question of nuclear safeguards and security of nuclear weapons, the necessary protocols have to be worked out and formalised – the sooner the better. Otherwise, we may well be confronted with a situation such as the one in Pakistan, in which deliberate proliferation of nuclear weapons technology was meekly condoned and the concerned person allowed to go scot free! In the case of nuclear weapons, it will be suicidal for any country to set its national interest and the reputation of its premier nuclear scientist above the safety of the world at large. I believe that in the matter of nuclear 'safety', nothing should be left to chance. If laxity is permitted in such matters, weapons of mass destruction could even find their way into the hands of terrorists and other such non-state parties with perverse ideologies or insane motives of their own. There is also the possibility of a leader enjoying unbridled power, unleashing weapons of mass destruction on another country to feed his megalomaniacal ego. This possibility becomes more probable when we recall that the USA, the sole superpower, turned a Nelson's eye in the case of deliberate proliferation of nuclear weapons technology by a Pakistani scientist because that country was their ally in the war on terrorism! Permissiveness in nuclear matters can endanger the entire world. In this regard, the superpower and the Nuclear Weapon States have a vital role to play. Approval of the Indian Parliament in May 2005 of 'The Weapons of Mass Destruction and their Delivery Systems – Prohibition of Unlawful Activities Bill', is a clear indication of India's concern for nuclear non-proliferation.

Before we conclude this chapter, let us turn to the field of sports and games and see what we attempted to do in the new century to improve India's performance in competitive sports at the international/world level. It is no secret that every Indian was ashamed at our abysmal performance in the Sydney Olympics, 2000. India, with a population of over one billion people, won only one Bronze Medal! We, in the Defence Forces, resolved to do something about the matter. The proposals for the establishment of the Army Institute of Sports (AIS) were initiated. The Defence Ministry was entirely supportive and allotted such funds as we asked for. AIS has now come up in Pune and the infrastructure created therein and the facilities available for sportspersons are of very high quality. We also reverted to our earlier sports policy under which competitions were held from unit level upwards rather than at the level of large formations or regimental centres to give maximum exposure to sports talent already available in the Army. We also embarked on a deliberate programme of talent scouting and bringing in gifted young people into the Army with reasonable incentives. We have nominated sports 'nodal' centres' for the development of specific sports at the Army level and support these nodes in the same manner as the AIS which is also the nodal centre for a number of events. With these measures and the employment of top-level international coaches, I am confident that our sports performance in the Beijing Olympics, 2008, will be better than any of our previous performances at the Olympic Games. While the Services will spare no pains to excel in the chosen sports disciplines, I must confess that I am disturbed by the kind of politics which seems to afflict our sports federations and governing bodies. While casting no aspersion on their patriotism, I fear that unfairness in selection of teams, sharing of coaches and infrastructure and selective inattention to providing potential 'Olympians' with international competitive experience, unless they belong to a favoured state or class of people, are likely to nullify all the efforts and break the spirit of our sportsmen. It is for the Government of India, Ministry of Sports, to look into the Augean stables of sports federation politics and cleanse them of the prevailing corruption. If my instincts do not lie, I fear that very drastic measures will be needed to set Indian sports on an even playing field. I believe that a constitutional amendment to make 'sports' a 'concurrent' subject if not a 'central' subject, the dissolution of sports bodies which are dragging Indian sports to the nadir, and promoting the cult of 'elitism' among our sports persons (a la singers and actors) are certain measures which must be taken to make India sports-conscious and give Indians the joy of hearing their National Anthem being played repeatedly at forthcoming Olympiad venues.

Let me share a passing thought which the readers may find suggestive. Atmospheric pollution in Delhi was very high once. It was caused by many sources such as polluting industries within the city, a thermal power plant with inadequate arrangements for precipitation of particulate matter, automobiles – specially buses, lorries and auto-rickshaws. Citizens suffered and choked in Delhi's noxious atmosphere. Ultimately, Public Interest Litigation (PIL) had to be resorted to. The Delhi High Court issued time bound orders for the polluters to take specified remedial measures. There was disbelief initially as to whether the Court's order would be carried out. There were petitions and appeals. But, the Court stood firm. The orders were obeyed. Today, Delhi has become far less polluted than it used to be. For our State Olympic Associations and National Sports Federations, which are protected by the Societies' Registration Act and which we believe are the root cause of the malaise that grips Indian sports, will some public spirited citizens not agitate the Courts with one or more PILs? If the

Associations and Federations were formed to nurture various sports, and all that they have achieved is the degradation of Indian sports, should they not be superseded or dismissed? Dear Reader, please think about this. Or you may never hear India's National Anthem from the Olympic stands.

From counter-insurgency operations to sports, from terrorist actions to disaster relief, from corruption in Defence procurements to training for war, from higher Defence Organisation to nuclear safeguards, we have traveled a rather 'choosy' route through the years 2001 and 2002, visiting only such stops as we wished to. The two years were, however, crammed with activities at every level and of every kind. It is not possible for me to do justice to all these in this book. Perhaps, you will bear with me and await the release of 'My Memoirs' to get the full details of all these events!

3

The Future of War

Karl von Clausewitz, Prussian military theorist (1780-1831), held that war is nothing but a continuation of politics by other means (*On War*, 1834). Few will question the essential validity of this statement. Likewise, Clausewitz's formulation that the object of war is to compel the enemy to submit to our will, is universally accepted. Throughout recorded history, we find instances of how nations sought to impose their wills on other nations by use of military force, making 'war' an essential feature of their international dealings. Every century has had its share of wars – wars for territory, for economic gains, to 'punish' another state, to defend one's religion and even, because of a woman as was the case in the Trojan War. However, the 20th century must rate as the bloodiest of all times, on account of the nearly 200 million deaths attributable to its wars, the exponential increase in the destructive power of weapons and, sadly, in the depravity displayed by many nations and peoples. Did the belligerents in these wars achieve the aims for which they fought? Did the human toll produce results desired by the belligerents in terms of diplomatic, political, economic or territorial gains? If they did, perhaps there is a case for resorting to war as the ultimate means available to a state to secure its national interests. If not, we need to examine the future of war as such in the new millennium, specially when weapons of mass destruction have become available in large numbers.

In this chapter we shall attempt to evaluate the concept of war in the light of socio-military circumstances prevailing today and arrive at some direction posts for mankind to follow in the future.

War is defined as 'a state of open, armed, often prolonged conflict, carried on between nations or states'. Sun Tzu's 'Art of War' ascribes critical importance to warfare and states, "Warfare is the greatest affair of state, the basis of life and death, the way to survival or extinction. It must be thoroughly pondered and analysed".

A war may consist of a number of campaigns which are its discrete segments. Campaigns may consist of one or more battles which are episodes of combat between the belligerents, of limited duration, for specific objectives and with a more restricted participation than in the campaign or war. Prior to the formation of agriculture based permanent settlements, our primitive ancestors engaged in continual inter-group rivalry for a variety of reasons such as to secure the use of richer hunting grounds, to capture women, for revenge against another group and so on. Though these were bloody enough strifes, they are not classified as 'war'. They may, instead, be termed as 'conflicts'. 'Conflicts' metamorphosed into 'wars' when our ancestors permanently settled on tracts of land chosen by them, resorted to agriculture and animal husbandry and began to store their surpluses of food for lean periods and value their flocks and herds highly enough to fight against these being driven off by invaders. These wars tended to be seasonal and the short period between successive crops was, perhaps, the most convenient 'campaigning period' for our agriculture-dependent ancestors.

From early agricultural settlements, through a process of interaction involving, inter alia, trade, cross-marriages, mutual aid against one another's adversaries and so on, the agrarian communities coalesced into small city-states and eventually into nation-states which exist even today. There is no reason to believe that the present day world order based on nation-states, will be superseded by some other dispensation such as 'regional' groupings. And the nation-state system provides the ideal environment for wars today.

We have so far used the term 'war' to encompass various types of human conflict. There are many types and natures of conflict which are referred to frequently as 'war'. A few such are cold war, proxy war, war against terror, war against drugs and so on. However, we use the term 'war' in the manner of our definition earlier as a state of open, armed conflict between nations.

Wars may be fought by nations for a variety of reasons. Common among these are wars to settle territorial disputes, to acquire valuable resources or deny these to the adversary, to achieve freedom from foreign rule or tyranny, to gain access to the seas, to ensure freedom of movement through international waters/canals, to effect forcibly a change in another country's leadership, to impose one's own national values on another, to punish a country for some action, to promote one's religion or defend one's religion, to garner huge profits for one's military-industrial-commercial complex and so on. One or more of these 'reasons' has been at the root of most wars fought till date. Perhaps, as the

Information Age progresses, cyber-space will become the latest arena where wars may be fought for altogether different reasons than what we have listed. Be that as it may, the beginning of all wars can be traced to the inability of leaders and diplomats of the belligerent countries to effectively communicate with each other and a weakening of the desire to live in peace. Leaders increasingly try to paint the adversary in the blackest colours and the whole nation is subjected to sustained pro-war propaganda. Efforts of peace-makers are stymied by adopting intransigent positions on issues involved, till war appears to be the only option left for the resolution of the inter-state problems. Bellicose leaders, incompetent diplomats, ineffective mediators, strident media and a gullible people constitute the explosive mixture that often leads to war. During the course of the ensuing war, the issues involved are often relegated to the back-burner pending its outcome. An outright victory will probably give the victors all that they sought while an adverse result will leave them worse off than they were earlier. And as so often happens, if the war ends in a stalemate, both sides will be left with increased mutual hostility and a large tally of casualties and damages. In the light of socio-military conditions prevailing in the world today, wars are more often than not, likely to end in stalemate with hardly any worthwhile result being achieved. Let us see what these conditions are.

The increasing interdependence of countries on one another, consequent to progressive economic globalisation is the first major reality that we have to face. War in any part of the world will impact the economic and commercial interests of a host of other countries. The USA's successive wars against Iraq (Gulf Wars 1 and 2) forced all those nations which were dependent on Arab oil to pay more for oil and its transportation. All these countries (and that constitutes the major part of the world community) were eager for the war to end so that they may pursue their economic interests as hithertofore. Their clamour would certainly have been factored into the decision of the US to end the war.

The lethality of modern weapons is another factor that will contribute to wars becoming shorter and more indecisive in future. No Great Power is likely to countenance two nuclear weapon states engaging in a prolonged war and exposing the region, and indeed, the world, to the possibility of nuclear exchanges with disastrous consequences, spread far and wide. It is to be expected that one or more of the Great Powers will compel the belligerents to stop fighting and start talking. As a result, wars between nuclear weapon states will necessarily end before any war aim can be realised. The situation in South Asia is a case in point. An India-Pakistan war will provoke the USA, Russia, China, the ASEAN countries, Europe, the UN and others to cry halt to the fighting as it could endanger the safety of the world. It is unlikely that their clamour will be ignored by either country though, to satisfy some weird notion of national pride, each may wait for the other to halt hostilities first! It is our belief that in the case of neo-nuclear weapon states, the superpower and other Great Powers will do their utmost to prevent wars between any two of them as, once started, the dynamics of war may bring one or the other country to the brink of defeat in a very short time and an 'in extremis' use of nuclear weapons may take place.

The age-old resort to making war in order to gain territories or colonies is, definitely passé; so too are the economics driven invasion of a small neighbour such as the Iraqi invasion of Kuwait. Wars to forcibly bring about a regime change in another country, punitive wars and wars to garner profits for one's military-industrial-commercial complex are still possible, but only for the superpower, as was demonstrated by the USA in case of Iraq and Afghanistan. And yet, whether the USA's aims of these wars have been achieved or not is a moot point. They appear to have won these wars but have not won the peace. It is only when peace returns that they may be able to reckon what dividends have accrued to them from these wars.

Internal wars within unsettled countries will continue, causing immense bloodshed and misery to their peoples. There will, perhaps, always be fratricidal wars in countries such as Sudan, Somalia and Congo as the countries which sell weapons and munitions to them, make handsome profits from these sales, no matter how much misery this causes to the tribally organised peoples of the affected countries. Sadly, the peoples of these countries seem to be unable to find a 'modus vivendi' and appear condemned to fight one another endlessly for no tangible benefit at all. After long years of purposeless fighting and with their people riven by diseases like AIDS, these countries will become easy prey to those coveting their natural resources and minerals.

Will 'civilizations' clash as Samuel P. Huntington has postulated? Will there be clashes among "the Western, Confucian, Japanese, Islamic, Hindu, Slavic-Orthodox, Latin American and possibly African civilizations" as Huntington wrote in '*Foreign Affairs*, Summer 1993'? Will a climacteric war eventually be fought between 'the West and the Rest'? Or, will the 'First, Second and Third Waves' which constitute three contending 'super' civilizations of our world today as postulated by Alvin and Heidi Toffler in *War and Anti-War,* fall upon one another in an orgy of violence, exposing humanity to 'extreme turbulence' and danger?

Both Huntington and the Tofflers have made out closely reasoned and logical theses. It is difficult to be categoric when one casts a vote for Huntington's or Tofflers' theories. The best one can say is that both theories are tenable, both are possible and both contain within them, many parts of the jigsaw puzzle that our fractured world has become today.

Tofflers' 'Theory of Trisection' seeks to explain the seeming resurgence of religion as a reaction to the injustices and frustrations heaped over a long period of time by nations belonging to one civilizational wave upon another. Thus, agrarian First Wave nations would resent their exploitation by the industrial Second Wave nations of the West and as a backlash, fall back on religious fanaticism or racial chauvinism or Marxist authoritarianism. In a similar manner, industrialised Second Wave countries are smarting at being left far behind economically by the knowledge based economies of Third Wave countries. The result again is a reversion to religious fanaticism, Marxism or ultra-nationalism.

We see disturbing indications of this kind of backlash in the world today. Religious fanaticism and obscurantism are encountered in every part of the world. Almost all religions have been affected by this phenomenon. If one group massacres persons of a different faith, there is another obscurantist cult which commits ritual mass suicide. There are examples of missionaries being accused of forcible religious conversions and of the brutal murder of some of them. There is intra-religious, inter-sect blood-letting and places of worship are often attacked. And above all, there are calls for religious wars – crusades, 'jehad', or whatever one may call it. These are throw-backs to the Dark Ages and bode ill for the future of humanity. Similarly, we see examples of ultra-nationalism as shown by the immigration laws of some countries and in the protection extended to domestic agricultural and industrial products against all competition, in total violation of international agreements. And there is the unedifying display of racial/national superiority in the actions of the superpower as shown in their treatment of prisoners and repeated callousness to what they call 'collateral' casualties. As we observed earlier, these are throwbacks to a more primitive time in human evolution. The Tofflers' formulation never seemed as valid as this before we started looking at the current world picture.

One point needs to be considered. That is the change that has been taking place over the centuries in the psyche of man. Over the millennia, humanity has evolved from the 'primitive' to the present level of 'civilisation'. However, this process has been attended by some undesirable consequences. The rich and the powerful have generally become extremely self-centred and indifferent to the needs and sensitivities of those who are less fortunate. The latter category too have developed undesirable traits such as impatience, intolerance and a propensity for violence, among others. The two opposite ends of the civilisational continuum, the rich and powerful (modern) and the less developed (primitive) seem destined to be perpetually in a state of mutual confrontation. The present manifestation of this phenomenon is in the form of terrorism of all kinds against the superpower and her allies. It is not difficult to visualise how the situation may develop in the future. We apprehend that one or more groups of terrorists or terrorist states may acquire Weapons of Mass Destruction (WMD) and 'challenge' the advanced countries using terrorist modus operandi backed up by WMD. This will inevitably lead to a war of great ferocity and lethality endangering the survival of humanity and damaging the eco-sphere irretrievably. It will be Armageddon.

How does humanity prevent this disaster? It is our belief that though the downslide into the abyss appears to be swift and unstoppable, it can be slowed down and halted in time. For this, we set out a few simple measures which would arrest the slide and give enough time to the statesmen of the world to set about reversing the trend. The measures that we suggest as immediate correctives are given below:

- Make the UN a more meaningful organisation rather than what it has become today – a fiefdom of the rich and powerful nations, headed by the USA. Perhaps this could be done by restructuring the UN to give the poorest of nations too a voice in matters affecting them and breaking the 'divine' right of the advanced countries to thrust their decisions on to the poor nations.
- Check arbitrariness by the Great Powers by giving greater scope for the UN General Assembly to nullify the effect of a Security Council vote or veto on any resolution touching the interests of the poorer nations if that vote or veto runs counter to their interests.
- Increase the role of the UN in monitoring the manufacture, sale and re-sale of various types of weapons, ranging from automatic rifles and carbines to weapons of mass destruction. Perhaps a UN monitoring agency with its own surveillance organisation including electronic and satellite surveillance means, coupled with a system of permanent 'on site' UN monitors in major arms manufacturing facilities backed up by randomly assigned roving teams of UN inspectors, should be

created. Also, a UN International Arms Sales/Resales Register should be opened and all member-nations should be required to enter full details of arms sales on line into the register, verifiable by UN on-site/roving monitors. The precise arrangements for such a monitoring programme will need to be worked out by experts so that it gives the UN complete control of the manufacture and spread of weapons in a reliable manner.

- The concept of an Enforcement Wing of the UN may be explored. We suggest that this wing should consist of high UN officials who are empowered to recommend penalties/sanctions against offending members to the Security Council to bring them to compliance with UN directives. Raising of an armed element with very high grade fighting capability, mobility and communication systems will also be useful to give 'teeth' to the UN's directions. As of now, even a nucleus does not exist. The entire idea, therefore, needs to be worked out 'ab initio'.

- A great deal needs to be done to control the proliferation of weapons of all types, ranging from weapons of mass destruction and their means of delivery to offensive, conventional weapons including bomber/multi-role aircraft, conventional artillery beyond a specified caliber and range and conventional missiles. No doubt all this sounds like a 'pipe-dream' but unless we place severe checks on offensive weapons (ideally, eliminate them), there will always be some country or the other which will be tempted to use these to achieve its aims. It needs to be noted that these offensive weapons, if acquired by non-state terrorist / outlaw organizations or a state on the brink of 'failure', would pose a grave threat to the safety and security of humanity.

- Terrorist groups acting out of various motivations are a major threat to peace in the world, and must be eliminated. We believe that the 'Bush Doctrine' of using what amounts to 'terrorist measures' to secure their elimination, is faulty and will aggravate the problem instead of solving it. Terrorists are groups of persons with grievances so grave that they resort to unlawful activities to publicise their case and leverage a favourable solution to their problems. It is only a fraction of the terrorist population of the world which is committed enough to seek self-annihilation rather than a favourable solution. Such people apart, we believe the causes of terrorism need to be identified and through concerted action (world-wide, if need be), eliminated step by step over a period of time. All the while, governments of countries facing terrorism, must continue to carry out operations to contain the menace and prevent further accretions to terrorist actions. Clearly, the 'winning of hearts and minds' of their own populace must become an article of faith with such governments.
- Globalisation of the economies of the world is turning out to be a new breeding ground for discontentment among many countries, specially those countries that are euphemistically termed as 'developing' countries. The richer and relatively more advanced nations must realise that an iniquitous or exploitative approach by them will, perhaps, benefit them only in the short term. In the longer term, their policies will boomerang on them in many forms such as violence against their people, properties and businesses in the developing country, organised (may be state-sponsored) terrorism against the exploiters and an escalating sequence of

violence-repression-violence, 'ad nauseam'. The World Trade Organisation (WTO) must ensure, by reviewing its various agreements, that exploitative clauses are removed and all nations are allowed 'a level playing field' for their economic and trade engagement with the rest of the world.

- Apart from enlightened economic cooperation among the nations of the world, worldwide capability must be bestowed on the UN to carry out worldwide watch for disasters of various types and to be able to react without delay to any developing situation, be it a deadly epidemic like AIDS or fire, flood, famine, various types of storms, tidal waves, earthquakes, volcanic eruptions and so on. Such an UN role will bring it as close as it is possible, to the idealist's concept of a World Government.

We have examined here the future of war as a major occupation of the nations of the world. We briefly surveyed how war as a concept originated, the various reasons for which wars are fought, the likelihood of more wars ending in stalemate rather than in a clearly positive or negative outcome and the reasons thereof. We have also examined the theories of Huntington and the Tofflers and while broadly endorsing their observations, suggested that human psyche probably develops in a cyclical pattern from the primitive, to the semi-civilized, the civilized, the decadent and back again to the primitive. We have expressed apprehension that humanity may be heading towards a climacteric clash between the 'Primitive' and the 'Modern' and suggested various measures which could stave off this contingency.

Despite everything we have said before and even after all our energies are directed towards preventing war, there will always be wars as long as there are nation-states and sentiments such as national honour, self-respect, adoration of heroism and the heady euphoria of victory. However, the effort to make wars rare, must continue. The great former US President Franklin Delano Roosevelt had put it succinctly in a speech in 1945: "More than an end to war, we want an end to the beginnings of all wars". That should be the direction of our endeavours. However, as H.L. Mencken observed in '*Notebooks*' (1956): "War will never cease until babies begin to come into this world with larger cerebrums and smaller adrenal glands". Till that distant future in human evolution, let us ponder over and analyse war and prepare to face any that may fall to our lot with courage and resolution.

4

Wars of the Future

When we examined the future of War, we came to the conclusion that long wars are unlikely, though short wars may continue to take place. The caveat was that nuclear weapon states will not be allowed to fight a war, specially the small countries whose very existence may be threatened by an adverse outcome in that war. However, it is not necessary that the Great Powers and other concerned countries will always be able to prevent such neo-nuclear states from fighting a short war though it is almost certain that they will be able to prevent nuclear weapons being used by either of the belligerent countries. In fact, we believe that the mere threat of use of nuclear weapons will cause decisive intervention on the part of the Great Powers and bring the war to an abrupt end, satisfactory to neither belligerent. Let us study one such war by means of a hypothetical scenario involving two neighbours, both neo-nuclear states, both classifiable as developing countries and both with a history of having fought a few indecisive wars in the course of last 50 years or so. Let us visualise a story taking shape in the year

2008 when relations between Nations 'A' and 'B', the two hypothetical neighbours, have again reached a breaking point over a long-standing dispute on the sharing of waters of a river, vital to both of them.

'A', the lower riparian country, wrongly perceives that 'B' has been illegally using up 'A's share of the waters. It has not been able to develop as successfully as 'B' and has serious problems of debt servicing. In fact, at one stage it came to the verge of defaulting on interest payments but this was averted through the munificence of her 'patron' Great Power who bailed it out at the eleventh hour. The bail-out package had a price tag as was expected. It involved stationing of foreign troops in a part of 'A' and virtual surrender of its freedom of action in foreign policy and economic matters. The citizens of 'A' generally resented the terms imposed by its benefactor but were acquiescent. However, the political opponents of the regime in 'A' made a major issue of it and virtually brought the country to a standstill through strikes and other industrial actions. State repression followed and riots ensued. Bomb blasts in public places and sectarian clashes took place. The situation was almost anarchical, but not quite so, as the regime in 'A' enjoyed the support of the armed forces. The government in 'A' decided that it was vital to divert the people's attention from the internal situation by embarking on a war with their arch enemy, 'B'. A possible 'casus belli' was the river waters dispute.

'B' was quite used to the manner in which successive regimes in 'A' ran their country. The river waters dispute, according to them, was a 'hoary chestnut' to be activated whenever the regime in 'A' was in 'deep waters'. This had happened a number of times before. After each period of tension, a Joint Commission would meet and hold a series of meetings in each other's country. Perhaps as a result of mutual 'looking after' or, because there was nothing wrong that was being done by 'B', both sides would agree to carry out some totally unnecessary studies and, in a bureaucratic manner, file and forget the issue for the time being. Something similar to that was going on in early 2008 when the curtain rises on our scenario.

'A' decided that a surprise attack on 'B', ostensibly to secure a 'headworks' some 30 km upriver from the border would be their opening gambit. If they succeeded in the surprise attack as they hoped they would, their people will be buoyed up by the victory and the opposition rendered 'toothless'. As to 'B', it would react violently to the attack but may not open another front for fear of offending the lodger Great Power. What was considered likely by the General Staff of 'A' was that 'B' would launch its forces against the troops of 'A', holding the bridgehead at the headworks and raise a hue and cry about the attack in the UN and internationally. It may, at the worst, use its Air Force against bases from where 'A's Air Force had supported the surprise attack, and possibly task her Navy to blockade 'A'. The General Staff had taken these likely reactions of 'B' into consideration and planned accordingly. They had ensured that they had adequate reserves of armaments, ammunition, fuels of all types and spare parts for their aircraft, ships and fighting vehicles. In addition, all air bases and forward air fields were well defended and the entire air space of 'A' had been covered by a mix of static and mobile radars so that enemy aircrafts are detected in time. Their airborne early warning aircraft as well as maritime strike aircraft were maintained at 100 per cent serviceability and their crews were well trained. Over and above all this, their 'lodger' patron invariably passed on to them details of 'B's military movements towards their border. In all, 'A' was satisfied that they had few vulnerabilities for 'B' to exploit, in case it decided to carry out a surprise attack against the headworks, 30 kilometers, inside the territory of 'B'. This it did on the night of the ongoing harvest festival in 'B'.

The 'coup de main' assault by its Special Forces carried out by helicopters and supported by gunships and fighter bomber aircraft was a complete success. There was no indication that any form of attack was planned by 'A', leave alone this bold attack on the headworks. 'B' recovered quite quickly from the surprise it had suffered and launched Rapid Reaction Forces against the enemy at the headworks. Simultaneously, 'B' launched air attacks against 'A's forward air bases and engaged some intruding aircraft in its airspace, bringing down one aircraft. Buoyed up by the spectacular success, 'A' gave clearance to its land forces to carry out shallow attacks (within four to six kilometers of the border) against four previously selected objectives on the lateral road, running parallel to the border on 'B's side. These tasks had been well studied and the troops to carry out the attacks had been repeatedly rehearsed elsewhere for their missions. Of the four attacks, each assessed at Brigade strength, two succeeded while one was beaten back with heavy casualties to the attacker. The fourth attack ran into serious difficulty as they lost direction and attacked a heavily fortified position, protected by minefields and well supported by artillery. There were a large number of casualties and some 90 soldiers were captured by 'B's forces. The remainder were asked by their controlling Headquarters to fall back on the firm base. By about midnight, 'A' had secured in all, three lodgements inside 'B' – the headworks, a cross-road some 50 kilometers south of the headworks and a piece of high ground some 20 kilometers to its north. They had lost an estimated 250 personnel, killed or wounded and some 90 soldiers had been taken prisoners. They had lost one fighter aircraft and two of their forward airfields were temporarily put out of use. 'B's ground positions were as already described when listing 'A's gains. Their casualties were fewer – some 30 personnel killed and 60 wounded. Their aircraft were unscathed and by midnight had made repeated attacks on 'A's airfields and points on their lines of communications.

At a little after mid-night, 'B's permanent representative in the UN apprised the Secretary General of the unprovoked attacks by 'A' and sought UN intervention to compel 'A' to halt its aggression without delay and withdraw its forces to its side of the border. 'B' also put into action a well thought out plan of retalliatory attacks, each with a force of two battalions to a brigade plus a battalion at a number of choke points on the enemy's lines of communications. All these attacks were supported by fighter ground attack aircraft, tanks, artillery and multi-barreled rocket launchers. The firepower developed was enormous and 'B's troops gained four out of the six objectives attacked without difficulty. They were partially successful on the fifth objective and were beaten back in the case of the sixth. Their casualties included 14 killed, 30 wounded and four persons believed to have been wounded and captured alive. 'B's naval forces delivered a devastatingly accurate, long range strike with missiles on the principal naval base and commercial harbour of 'A'. The efforts of both maritime strike aircraft as well as air force aircraft to engage the naval task force firing the missiles, were unsuccessful. By daybreak, 'B' had inflicted sufficient punishment on 'A' for the latter to lose its early sense of euphoria. They had three enemy lodgments in their territory –

one in depth and two close to the border. In turn, they had secured four shallow depth lodgments in 'A's territory. They had also the confidence that the UN will blow the whistle on hostilities within 24 hours.

The next morning, the UN Security Council passed a resolution calling for an immediate ceasefire and for troops to go back to their own side of the borders within the next 48 hours. What was galling to the leaders of 'A' was that the unanimous resolution named 'A' as the 'aggressor' and even their patron Great Power had endorsed it. These developments could not be kept from the media, which (both national and foreign, print as well electronic) broke the news to the world at large as to how 'A', for some trumped up reason, committed armed aggression against its neighbour and had come off second best in the fighting. 'A's leadership was thoroughly discredited and forced out of power by public clamour. Troops were pulled back to their sides of the border and the war ended within 48 hours.

The events in the scenario we have painted for our discussion, have been deliberately exaggerated and speeded up. Perhaps, reality may move at a different pace and in a somewhat different direction. However, for learning what may happen when two neo-nuclear neighbours decide to fight and the possible contours of such a war, the scenario we have painted will suffice. Let us see what we can learn from the unfortunate experiences of 'A' and 'B' in their absurd war.

We first turn to 'A's war plans. It had some laudable features which make for success not only in short wars but in all types of wars. These are:

- *Surprise:* A war launched from 'cold start' will achieve surprise as opposed to one which involves elaborate preparation, massing of forces and building up forward stocks and so on. This should not be taken to mean that these preparations can be neglected. Far from it. These need to be built into our peace-time posture which, while not being overtly aggressive, must cater for readily available peacetime forces undertaking offensive operations with carefully located and stocked logistic facilities. 'Cold start' operations will run out of steam relatively early. Care must, therefore, be taken to assign them tasks within their capability. Follow up forces should be catered for to maintain momentum and achieve deeper objectives and should this not be possible within a very short period, the depth of the objectives will need to be tailored suitably.

- *Synergy:* 'Cold start' operations, more than any other, demand synergy among the three Services from the very beginning. Classical modes of application of Air Force will have to be modified to support the vital Cold Start Ground Forces actions. This would entail allocation of adequate close air support effort at the very start of the fighting. Without question, counter air operations must go on even at that stage but they may 'peak' somewhat later than they would otherwise.

- *Coup-de-Main Forces*: Bold employment of airborne, helicopter-borne and air landed forces will achieve not only physical success but moral ascendancy as well. While the designated objective will fall (as in this case), a far greater effect will be created on the enemy's decision makers. They are likely to need more time to make a balanced decision and even then, there is likelihood of their decision being tinged with caution or worse, militarily unjustifiable haste as a result of political needling. When war starts, even if it starts with a reverse, matters military must be left to the military; political meddling is a sure recipe for disaster. In the instant case, 'B' appears to have avoided this pitfall.

- *Selection of Objectives*: Barring the headworks, the other objectives selected by 'A' were shallow in depth with reference to the border and spaced well apart. This helps to divide enemy's reaction forces and, in post war talks, gives 'A' a 'trading chip'. Further, only shallow penetrations can be logistically sustained from existing facilities unless one resorts to air maintenance which is very expensive or, makes elaborate arrangements for logistics during peace time, risking loss of surprise.
- *Assured Availability of Major Assets*: 100 per cent availability state for prime war fighting assets such as airborne early warning aircraft and maritime strike aircraft, together with adequate maintenance spares was catered for. This would pay rich dividends in war against enemy's Air and Naval forces.

These were some of the positive features of 'A's war plans. These plans were, however, not 'thought through' to finality as is evident from even the D-Day actions. The defects in 'A's plans are:

- *Faulty Aim*. 'A's aim in the war was to divert domestic attention from the non-performance and failure of its Government and ensure its survival. In the event, precisely the opposite was achieved. The regime fell. Our conclusion is that the aim was not a legitimate war aim. War, though it may create 'fog' in relation to matters military, does exactly the opposite on matters political. Motivations of states (governments) become clearer as a result of war. 'A' could not have hoped to obfuscate the failure of their Government to perform by starting the war. Let us assume that 'A' was forced to go to war because 'B' was denying it water for irrigation and its crops were withering or could not be sown; that despite protracted negotiations and agitating the matter in the UN and the International Court of Justice, they received no satisfaction; there would have been legitimacy in going to war for 'A'. This was not, however, the case. The conclusion we derive from this is that the aim of war must be for securing 'vital' as opposed to 'frivolous' interests. War may be resorted to if no other means are available to achieve the vital aim.

- *Assessment of Enemy's Likely Reactions*: The planners in 'A' were guilty of underestimating 'B's reaction to their attack. They assumed that both the Air Force and Navy of 'B' will be restrained by the presence of the 'lodger' Great Power to selective air attacks and a naval blockade. They should have taken into consideration their enemy's full range of capabilities and catered for the same. This kind of grievous error arises because they tried to appreciate their enemy's 'intention' instead of his capabilities. In all military planning, it will be wise if the full range of capabilities of the adversary are carefully assessed and catered for, in the contingency plans. Attempt to 'read' the enemy's 'intention' is a difficult exercise because it is highly subjective, likely to be coloured by wishful thinking and not based on irrefutable logic or evidence. On the other hand, capabilities can be clearly identified and can, therefore, be guarded against.

- *Aggression Unsupportable*: Whatever be the relationship between a Great Power and a country that has committed aggression without concurrence of the former, the Great Power will find it extremely difficult to support the aggressor before the UN Security Council. 'A's discomfiture in the Security Council was only to be expected.

We have seen how a hypothetical war may start and end within a very short time in the years ahead when the belligerents are neo-nuclear states. In fact, it is considered highly unlikely that two neo-nuclear states will embark on a war, knowing fully well that the rest of the world and specially the Great Powers will not allow it. The risks of one or the other belligerent, using or threatening to use a nuclear weapon, are great and the consequences could be catastrophic. It is, therefore, in the interest of these neo-nuclear states as indeed, of the whole world, that they work for the abolition of nuclear weapons from the world in a time-bound manner. A weapon so fearful that it cannot be used, cannot be permitted to remain in our arsenals because the terror it inspires keeps the peace in the world. If such a peace is broken just once, all humanity would be destroyed. The risks are far too great to be balanced by the claim of the proponents of nuclear weapons that no nuclear power has fought another war since these weapons were first made. If they do, it will be the final 'curtain' for mankind.

5

Intelligence for the 21st Century

Intelligence is all about knowledge. Knowledge is a state of awareness or knowing, gained through study, observation, perception, inference and similar processes. When knowledge in relation to a military or non-military problem is analysed, evaluated for accuracy and reliability, its relevance to our requirement is judged, and further when this processed knowledge is correlated with other bits of similarly processed knowledge relevant to the issue, it is called Intelligence. If we adapt the analogy of 'pure' science and 'applied' science, knowledge would be the former while Intelligence will approximate the latter. Another term which we commonly encounter is Information. This term is best treated as a raw material for Intelligence, a piece of knowledge which has not so far been processed in the manner we have just mentioned. The reason for this excursion into semantics will become clear when we examine the lacunae that exist in our intelligence apparatus.

In this chapter, we shall familiarise ourselves with various types of intelligence organisations, identify our major requirements of intelligence in the 21st century and suggest modifications or improvements in such organisations in India so as to meet the intelligence requirements more comprehensively and in a more timely manner.

Intelligence Organisations

In general terms, all intelligence work can be classified under two heads:

(a) Acquisition.

(b) Counter-intelligence.

Each of these two types of intelligence work is carried out at different functional levels in the country and in the armed forces. Broadly, these levels are national, strategic, operational or tactical. The last two terms, though more common in military usage, have their non-military equivalents at executive and functional levels. At each of these levels and at different times and circumstances, there are different intelligence requirements. The basic 'stock in trade' of the intelligence community in all cases remains 'Information'. However, the focus of attention of intelligence operators shifts from the 'General' to the 'Specific' and the 'Long Term' to the 'Immediate'. This variable focus based on specificity and immediacy together with the level of functioning and the nature of the intelligence work constitutes the basis of Intelligence organisations.

Two broad types of intelligence organisations could exist. These are monolithic organisations and layered organisations. There could also be combinations of these two broad categories.

If one takes external intelligence, most countries have a monolithic organisation in which the entire responsibility for acquiring external intelligence is of one agency, for example, the Central Intelligence Agency of the USA or the British Secret Service (MI-6), the French DGSE, Mossad of Israel, Inter Services Intelligence (ISI) of Pakistan and Research and Analysis Wing (R&AW) of India. All these organisations are responsive to a central headquarters, which, in turn, derives its mission from the national leadership. In practice, however, these organisations operate almost autonomously. The head of such an agency often determines its thrust lines. In some cases, where the top leadership of the country has not given them clear directions, they could come up with 'skewed' intelligence based on the organisational head's predilections and lead the country on an unintended path. In most cases, however, what does happen is that the head of the external intelligence agency often becomes a powerful factor in national politics and enjoys rapport with the rulers.

Layered organisations are, on the other hand, organised to approximately parallel the political or military hierarchy and develop affiliations by virtue of proximity to the corresponding layers of the larger organisation. This effectively moderates their urge to follow an independent policy and encourages them to follow the 'official' line in their work. There are few external intelligence agencies which are layered. The character of external intelligence is such that it does not lend itself to layering except at the operational or tactical level. However, layering is a common practice in military intelligence organisations barring agencies like the Defence Intelligence Agency (DIA) of India or the USA which are monolithic.

Monolithic organisations have the advantages of positive central direction and control of intelligence operations, swift up and down communications which facilitate speedy passage of information and orders and, above all, a sense of greater commitment and participation in the affairs of state engendered by the relative freedom of action they enjoy.

Layered organisations, on the other hand, are relatively slow moving, bureaucratic and display less dynamism and commitment as compared to the monoliths. However, their lateral affiliations enable them to be echelon-responsive and their product, consequently, is generally more readily usable at different levels.

There is no fundamental flaw in either type of organisation. Both types are current today and relied upon by their governments. Care must, however, be taken to see that they are staffed by the right kind of personnel who will always act in the country's interests and not follow an altogether divergent path.

A few more words about the architecture of intelligence organisations are necessary. Acquisition of intelligence is undertaken both outside and within the country. Counter-intelligence on the other hand is almost always carried out within the country. Often, the role of counter-intelligence and acquisition of intelligence within the country are entrusted to the same organisation such as the Intelligence Bureau in India. In rare cases, where a counter-intelligence organisation has to operate outside the borders of the country, orders enabling this are usually issued, such as in the case of our country.

Apart from the principal national level organisations which have been discussed, there are a number of intelligence organisations serving specialised government departments. The armed forces, central and state level police organisations, paramilitary forces, the department of revenue, the department of customs and excise, are some of the organisations which have well developed intelligence organisations. These are mostly acquisition oriented. However, the armed forces have well developed counter-intelligence organisations as well. Further, in order to more effectively support troops engaged on counter-insurgency operations, specialised units with high capability for acquisition of intelligence have been created. There are also regional internal security groups which cover the regions for which they have been raised and provide advance warning of any changes in the Internal Security situation in their regions. The modern state, therefore, has no dearth of intelligence organisations. How effective these organisations are, is the question. We shall examine this shortly at both the national and domestic levels.

Intelligence at the National Level

At the national level, the requirement of intelligence is of a strategic and long term nature. In relation to the armed forces, both strategic intelligence and operational intelligence are required. Countries need to know about their enemies, potential enemies, friends and neighbours. In fact, acquisition of intelligence about all these countries will be an important task for the national external intelligence agency. The intelligence required is about the 'target' country's politics, economics, military including strategic and operational plans, alliances, commerce and industry, communications, internal security situation, strategic plans and so on. In fact, there is hardly any aspect of the 'target' country which is not of interest to the policy makers of the 'home' country. As the necessary information is gathered in diverse ways, the 'home' country's analysts subject it to the full range of processing – starting with sifting 'the grain from the chaff,' rating its quality based on the reliability and reputation for accuracy of the source who fed in the information, relating it to kindred information already available in order to obtain a cross-check or corroboration or, in its absence discover whether any previously available information contradicts or negates the present input, interpreting the input and analysing its significance and effect on our plans, storing the intelligence into which the input has been now transformed, disseminating it to those concerned and finally, tasking the agency for further inputs if necessary. This entire process of extracting a nugget of intelligence from large masses of raw information is what 'Analysts' do at the headquarters of the external intelligence agency and at various in-between levels. They have to be experts on the target country, possess an instinctive 'feel' for what is valuable and be completely sincere and thorough in their analysis. Even a hint of wishful thinking or a desire to pander to their superior's predilections will vitiate the quality of the work they do – even to the extent of making it useless or, what is worse, dangerous. Above all the analysis must be done in time as dated intelligence is fit only for newspapers. Since we have dwelt at some length on the intelligence cycle, it may interest you to know what happens to the odd bits and pieces of information that flow in and do not connect up to give any useful deduction. These are not 'dumped' and forgotten, but are 'flagged' and retained for a long time till they connect up or they are proved to be valueless or irrelevant. The storage and retrieval system of the analyst must be of such versatility and capacity as to be able to do this. In the past, elaborate filing systems were created for this purpose. Today, computers have taken over this job. However, notwithstanding the capability of computers to store and facilitate retrieval of information and be able to process data as programmed, in the final analysis, there is no replacement in sight for the expert analyst who, over the years, develops an instinct for intelligence.

The actual process of acquisition of external intelligence is a subject by itself. The methods used range from 'open sources' or what is in the realm of public knowledge, having been published or aired over media, to espionage, from visual observation of a subject of interest to imagery from an intelligence satellite, from gossip and general conversation to eavesdropping on electronic circuits or radio interception, and various electronic and electro-optic methods using remote sensing techniques. It is not our intention to dilate here on these methods. However, two points deserve mention. The first is that 'open sources' provide the bulk of the information to the analyst about the target country. This alone should underline how important it is for the analyst to be an expert on his target country. The second point that must be made is that despite all the sophistication and wizardry of modern scientific aids to gather intelligence, there is no replacement in sight for the human agent – the old fashioned 'spy'. Espionage has often been referred to as the 'second oldest profession'. It would appear that it will continue to hold its pride of place in the foreseeable future as well.

We now move on to the work of national level intelligence agencies within the country. We shall discuss this under two broad heads – Acquisition and Counter-intelligence.

Intelligence agencies at the national level are numerous, if we also count those which are specific to specialised departments. However, from the general intelligence point of view, all countries have one single agency such as the British Security Service (MI-5), the

French Deuxiemme (2nd) Bureau, Israel's Shin Beth and India's Intelligence Bureau (IB). The primary aim of all these agencies is to detect, prevent, defeat or neutralise any form of threat to national security from within or from outside the country. The major threats that are focused on are subversion of loyalty of the people, incitement to secession, fomenting rebellion and various forms of internal disorder, sabotage of vital facilities and installations, espionage and threats to the security of national leaders. In many countries, the regime has thought it proper to task the national premier intelligence agency with the responsibility for political intelligence, specially in relation to the electoral fortunes of the ruling party and matters relating to public perceptions about their leaders. Whatever be the legitimacy of such tasking, it does tend to politicise the agency at different levels to the detriment of its professional performance.

Internal national level intelligence agencies are structured hierarchically with their echelons broadly paralleling major administrative echelons. At the apex, the organisation is controlled by the Interior or Home Ministry with a Director who has the rank of a Secretary to the government. He is usually a police officer though in many countries lawyers, military officers and even eminent civil servants have been known to have headed such organisations. Usually, every constituent state of the country (or group of states in the case of smaller states) has a representative with Additional Directors or Joint Directors heading it as in the case of our IB. The organisation usually goes right down to districts and sub-districts where we find Central Intelligence Officers or their Deputies.

In countries beset by a host of internal problems such as India, the premier internal intelligence agency, IB, has a vital role to play. With an ongoing proxy war in Jammu and Kashmir, long standing secessionist/sub-nationalist movements in the north-east, religious fanaticism, left wing extremism, illegal immigrants and our own unique brand of democratic politics, the IB has come to wield considerable influence in national affairs.

How do internal intelligence agencies operate? To answer this question very briefly, they operate in the classic police manner 'on the basis of information received'. The information is obtained through a string of spies and informers who disclose what they know, for a fee and undertake further inquiries – also for a fee. While some of these informants are no doubt from the criminal classes, a fair amount of information is obtained gratuitously from friends, well-wishers and politicians 'with an axe to grind'. But information does not get tainted because an unsavoury person divulges it. So long as one takes effective steps to guard against a 'double cross' and checks out all information received, one can derive much useful intelligence from it. Information is also gathered through attendance at public functions, meetings with various persons of interest, media – both national and regional, rumours, telephone tapping when authorised by law, interrogation of persons in custody, refugees, censorship of mail when in vogue and so on. The information gathered at grassroots level is filtered up, gathering as it were, weight from the interpretation process at each successive level, till at some stage the information gets accepted as fully processed intelligence for dissemination and action. In sum, the process of deriving intelligence domestically, is quite similar to that for external intelligence.

The counter-intelligence and security aspects of national level domestic intelligence constitute a major part of their charter of duties. Detection and defeating of espionage activities within the country, breaches of official promulgations relating to security of information, plans, materials and operations, anti-national activities of all kinds, whether by foreigners or own nationals, these are vital areas of concern to the agency. In fact, internal security of a nation depends to a great extent on how well its internal intelligence agency discharges its duties.

The Indian Perspective

India has entered the 21st century with a sense of eager anticipation for great achievements to come. Many Indians feel that the future holds promise of great progress and prosperity for India, happiness and a fuller life for its billion plus citizens. We too believe that greatness is in store for India and it will, in the next decade or two, assume a position of considerable importance among the comity of nations. To be able to attain what seems to be destined for us, we have to make sure that no obstacles come in the way of our smooth progress towards prosperity. War, pestilence, rebellion, terrorism, machinations of adversaries, hostile alliances and problems confronting our friends and allies are some of the obstacles or hazards which may slow our progress. It would be ideal if they could be detected at a very early stage and not allowed to mature into a direct or indirect threat to our national interests. In broad strategic terms, these threats constitute the essence of the intelligence acquisition plan at the national level.

The armed forces too, would be eager to learn the maximum about the strength, weapons, locations and possible modes of employment of our enemies' reserve forces, about key military plans including offensive, defensive and contingency plans and a host of relevant military strategic intelligence. Without burdening you with the minutiae of strategic military intelligence, we shall merely state that all matters military and technological circumstances bearing on the military are of great interest to our defence planners and it would be for the external intelligence agency (Research and Analysis Wing in our case) to seek and provide this intelligence.

In addition to what we have stated as being our national strategic intelligence requirements, there are numerous other government departments which need strategic intelligence inputs from across the world. Economists, industrialists, scientists, bankers, traders, engineers, doctors and so many categories of persons who constitute the 'backbone' of India, rely upon their controlling ministries to obtain all possible intelligence about their special areas of interest. This acquisition too falls within the province of R&AW. From all this, one can appreciate what a strong organisation the R&AW has to be to satisfy all its clients.

In terms of domestic national level intelligence, the IB has the responsibility for acquiring strategic and operational intelligence, bearing on the internal security of the nation. The proxy war, insurgencies in different parts of the north-east, Left Wing extremism, religious fundamentalism, regulation of the activities of foreigners within the country and intelligence relating to national borders where the Army is not deployed, are some of the major areas of IB's concern. In the foreseeable future, it is assessed that intelligence relating to the proxy war, insurgencies, Left wing extremism and communal matters will demand bulk of the IB's attention and resources.

With this brief review of the intelligence requirements in the 21st century, we can attempt an assessment of whether the existing apparatus is adequate or whether improvements in methods of working or structural changes or, both, are required to boost clientele satisfaction. However, we are neither in a position to nor permitted by security considerations to write about the positive achievements of our intelligence apparatus, barring what is already in the realm of public knowledge. The interception of a telephone conversation between Pakistan's Army Chief who was then in Beijing and one of his trusted colleagues in Islamabad was, indeed, an intelligence coup. That *one* intercept helped to blow sky-high the pretended innocence of Pakistan's Army establishment about their perfidious armed intrusion into the Kargil sector of Jammu and Kashmir, an intrusion that was to cost both countries a large number of casualties. Such coups generally are not publicised but the fact that this coup *did* occur should suggest that the Signal Intelligence Wing is functioning alright. However, the equipment with them is not of 'the state of the art' quality and is in insufficient numbers. Reliable direction finding equipment too is needed together with a major upgradation of our cryptanalysis capability, especially in respect of texts in certain important languages. Even in the counter-insurgency operations areas, Communication Intelligence has played a very important role in giving security forces advance notice of intended hostile actions, the state of morale of the terrorists, their problems, their internal differences, locations, chain of command and so on. All these pieces of information, duly processed at the appropriate level, give the security forces a great deal of help in dealing with the terrorists. Improvements in terms of better scanners, DF equipment and jammers for selective use together with improved cryptanalysis methods will make the Signal Intelligence Wing more potent.

In the field of other forms of Technical Intelligence such as Imagery Intelligence (IMINT), Electronic

Intelligence (ELINT) and Computer Intelligence, the story is similar. Our equipments and instruments need upgradation. Personnel manning these branches of intelligence are, however, first rate as can be judged from the very laudable results they have produced in the past with old equipment.

A word here about different agencies using the same equipment. Most of these items are of imported origin and costly. If R&AW has purchased a certain item, it should not be normally necessary for Military Intelligence (MI) or IB to purchase the same item. However, given the completely different focus of the R&AW, MI and IB, it is well nigh impossible for the same equipment to be shared by the three agencies or, for the agency which 'owns' the equipment to also cater for the requirements of the others. Some duplication is inevitable and, in many cases, desirable. Having regard to the task in hand, if in the interest of timeliness, user focus and ready availability, double or three times the cost of a piece of equipment has to be paid, so be it. We should not compromise on National Security requirements merely to save some money. Incidentally, a central committee was set up after the Kargil Review Follow-up Task Force on Intelligence recommended such a coordinating body for Technical Intelligence purchases. We are not aware of what that body has achieved. However, in an already difficult procurement system, to introduce yet another link in the chain, does not appear to be well advised.

We take up the requirements of Human Intelligence (HUMINT), which, arguably, is the most important branch of intelligence acquisition despite the technological upgradation of all other types of intelligence acquisition. In HUMINT, clear cut areas of responsibility, both in terms of jurisdictional area and level of intelligence have been laid down in the mandate for R&AW, IB, MI and so on.

External intelligence of all but tactical intelligence is the charge of R&AW. The Army acquires its own contact and battlefield intelligence through its combat units and somewhat longer range tactical or near-operational intelligence through its organic intelligence units. This arrangement predates even the founding of R&AW on 21st September, 1968. To enable R&AW to appreciate the intelligence requirements of the armed forces, a team of military officers headed by a Chief Military Intelligence Adviser (CMIA), forms part of R&AW. Notwithstanding this thoughtful arrangement, Military Intelligence requirements do not seem to get the kind of attention they deserve. There are finite limits to the number of military officers who could be posted to R&AW. To ask the military to accept greater time lag between a requisition for intelligence and its outcome is one answer which, the military cannot accept. Perhaps, MI could be mandated to acquire strategic and operational intelligence in respect of a few countries of great concern to the armed forces, in addition to the R&AW. Lest this recommendation creates a dichotomy in responsibility for strategic and operational intelligence, we must state that R&AW should continue to be the agency responsible. The MI mandate, if given, would merely result in readier response to requisitions and perhaps a better analysed product at the end of the intelligence cycle.

Mutual sharing of intelligence among intelligence agencies is poor, specially from the MI to the others. This should be set right through institutionised arrangements, perhaps under the aegis of the National Security Council Secretariat (NSCS) or through routine fortnightly briefings of the Chiefs of Staff Committee. Unfortunately, these briefings are handled half-heartedly and inappropriate representatives are frequently detailed by the civilian agencies. Sharing of intelligence on a regular basis is important to develop mutual understanding and confidence.

Likewise, the armed forces, as users of external and internal intelligence provided by the civilian intelligence agencies, must give a regular feed-back together with suggestions on how matters could be improved further. Regrettably, feedback from the services to the intelligence agencies has been the exception rather than the rule. This needs improvement.

A Defence Intelligence Agency (DIA) has been created in our country recently. Its charter of duties and its 'inter se' relationship with the intelligence agencies of the three services must be reviewed so that the utility of the DIA is maximised. One is encouraged to note that Net Assessment has been given due importance in the DIA. The DIA, as the nodal agency for Technical Intelligence for the services, must have functional control of all military satellites and its own electronic warfare aircraft and ships. Its imagery specialists must be the best that we have and need to be 'encadred' and given career protection. Its resources for exploiting open sources need to be enhanced and additional linguists authorised to it. We feel that this new organisation will be an asset to Chiefs of Staff Committee or CDS in times to come, if we nurture it carefully through its infancy.

Finally, a word about Intelligence in the Indian perspective. India is renowned as the home of savants such as Chanakya whose treatise on statecraft, *Arthashastra,* is considered a classic till today. By virtue of having a long and continuous history of over 5000 years, India has had to deal with Intelligence continuously over the centuries. Our human resources are second to none. If we select the most suitable persons for induction into the intelligence agencies and train them right, we should be serving our country well.

6

The Changing Face of Terrorism

Terrorism has been defined by the United States Government as "premeditated, politically motivated violence perpetrated against non-combatant targets by subnational groups or clandestine agents, usually intended to influence an audience". They also explain 'international terrorism' as "terrorism involving citizens or the territory of more than one country" and 'terrorist groups' as "those which practice or have significant subgroups, that practice international terrorism". India too had defined terrorism in Chapter II, Section 3(a) and (b) of the Prevention of Terrorism Act, 2002, (POTA), now repealed. The POTA said much what the Americans have said, but in 'legalese'. For ease of understanding, it will be preferable to use the American definition.

There are many laws and ordinances passed by different countries giving other definitions or amplifications of the terms 'terrorism', 'international terrorism' and 'terrorist act'. Most of these laws/ordinances are of late 20th century origin, suggesting that some event or events which took place during that period, forced countries to study and legislate against terrorism. Perhaps, it was the rash of hijacking of commercial airliners which took place during the period starting from 28th July, 1968, when an El Al aircraft, flying from Rome to Tel Aviv, was hijacked by three persons belonging to Popular Front for Liberation of Palestine (PFLP) to Algiers to obtain the release of 16 Arab prisoners in Israeli jails. The 16 prisoners were exchanged for the 25 Israelis who were on that flight and had been held hostage. The train of terrorist action closely followed by counter-terrorist reaction has continued without pause, ever since that infamous 28th July, 1968.

Apart from hijacking of aircraft, terrorists carried out a wide variety of terrorist actions. Some of these are the use of car bombs in crowded places, bombing of crowded departmental stores and government offices, abduction of diplomats and even an ex President of Argentina (who, sadly, was executed by the abductors), wanton destruction of hijacked airliners on the ground at Amman and Cairo, slaughtering of 25 passengers and wounding of 76 at the Tel Aviv airport, killing of tourists, setting off bombs in airliners in flight and so on. One of the more lurid terrorist actions took place on 5th September, 1972, when eight terrorists of the Black September group killed 11 Israeli athletes and coaches at the Munich Olympic Games. Five of the terrorists were also killed. We can continue this sad litany of terrorist crimes almost till the time this book goes to the press but we are still likely to have missed out on the 'latest' incident. The manifestations of terrorism have become so commonplace these days!

While acts of terrorism have no genuine justification, the retaliatory actions taken by the affected governments, have been equally beyond the pale of international law or even universally accepted practices. Destruction of 13 airliners owned by three Arab-owned airlines by Israeli commandos at Beirut on 28th December, 1968, was clearly illegal, though in retaliation to the 28th July, 1968, hijacking. Targeted assassinations of leaders with suspected terrorist connections, the June 1982 invasion of Lebanon in response to the wounding of Israel's Ambassador to Britain by the Black June group, the cruise missile attacks on the Al Shifa pharmaceutical plant in Khartoum and on suspected Osama bin Laden training camp in Afghanistan, ordered by the then US President Clinton in retaliation to the terrorist attacks on US embassies at Nairobi and Dar es Salaam – all these and many others clearly transcend whatever civilized nations believe to be legally permissible. It would appear that in the latter half of the 20th century, there was vigorous growth of terrorism and even more vigorous state reaction to terrorism. The cycle of violence-counter violence-violence has gone on, never abating, always escalating. It might be worthwhile to pause and analyse where this spiral of violence will lead humanity to. Perhaps, one should look (albeit briefly) into the reasons for the genesis of terrorism and see whether we can divine the direction which terrorism may take in the future and what we may do to eradicate it.

Despite the belief promoted by many stalwarts in the US Administration, terrorism is NOT a new phenomenon; and its date of birth is NOT 11th September, 2001. The Jewish Zealots' Caesaria Revolt against the Romans (AD 66-70) and the Roman reactions thereto indicate its religious origin. We see secular conquerors like Chenghiz Khan and Tamerlane employing terrorist methods to speed up their conquests. All they did was to massacre the inhabitants of captured cities and send word ahead of their forces that those who did not yield with alacrity would meet with the same fate.

Yet another secular example of terrorism is to be found in the second year of the French Revolution in France. The *guillotine* was kept so busy that the famous British politician, Edmund Burke, was compelled to call the new French dispensation, 'the Reign of Terror'. Russian anarchist Peter Kropotkin, who espoused the cause of mass terrorism, enunciated the basic plank of modern terrorism, the 'propaganda of the deed'. "Do it with bombs", he said. The failure of the European revolutions of 1848 to dislodge conservative governments led German anarchist Karl Heinzen to conclude that frontal attacks by revolutionaries against the state would not succeed. Instead, chaotic and confused conditions can be created through widespread and indiscriminate use of bombs which will paralyse the authorities and enable governments to be overthrown.

The 20th century, with the awakening of nationalist impulses such as the Zionist vision of creating a Jewish state in Palestine, rising Arab nationalism and the upsurge of suppressed ethnic minorities like Irish Catholics, gave a big fillip to the growth of terrorist organisations. Some of these which grew to full stature in the 20th century are: Irish Republican Army (IRA), Provisional IRA, Ulster Defence Association and Ulster Volunteer Force – all in Northern Ireland; Action Directe of France (1979), ETA of Spain (1950s), Turkey's Kurdistan Workers' Party - PKK (1984), Red Army Faction of Germany (1960), Red Brigades of Italy (1970); a number of Arab/Islamic terrorist organisations like PFLP of the 28th July, 1968 fame, Abu Nidal Organisation (1974), Black September (1970), Al Fatah (1957), Hamas (1987), Hezbollah (1978), Muslim Brotherhood, Al Qaida (1990); African groups like Eritrean Liberation Front of Ethiopia (1958), FLN of Algeria (1954), ZAPU and ZANU of Zimbabwe (1961); Asian groups like Aum Shinri Kyo of Japan (1987),

Japanese Red Army (1971); Harkat ul Mujahideen, JeI, JKLF, all of J & K; Lashkar e Taiba and Harkat ul Jehad e Islami (HUJI) of Pakistan; Moro Liberation Front of Philippines and LTTE of Sri Lanka (1972); American groups like the USA's Ku Klux Klan (reborn in 1920s), Canada's Quebec Liberation Front, the Shining Path of Peru (1969) and the Revolutionary Movement of October 8th of Brazil. This list reads almost like a directory of terrorist organisations but in actual fact, it is only a part list. There must surely be something seriously wrong with our world if so many countries have some people desperate enough to pick up weapons and fight organised governments for whatever cause they have chosen to espouse. Let us see if we can identify what ails the world and what makes some people and not all, turn to terrorism. This may lead us to conclusions regarding the likely face of terrorism in the 21st century.

Terrorism is the application of violence for the purpose of achieving some aim or goal. It is often the response of a person or group of persons, who have been alienated from their society or government and have suffered repression, harassment, humiliation and persecution. They are generally angry and frustrated and sometimes desperate to the point of being prepared to undertake suicidal missions for their cause. They usually suffer from low self-esteem due to the rough treatment their self-image and ego had received before they took to terrorism. They are generally keen to merge their individuality into their group and find some nourishment for their impoverished ego in group companionship and violence. There is no conclusive evidence to suggest that the ethnicity or religious beliefs of a person pre-dispose him to become a terrorist. In fact, judging from the occurrence pattern of terrorism the world over, with every religion and race producing its own crop of terrorists, the reverse may well be truer, that race and religion may not predispose a person towards terrorism. The reasons which do cause a person to take up terrorism are generally quite 'secular' reasons which could apply to any racial group, anywhere in the world. Of course, not every affected person becomes a terrorist. This requires a special individual psyche, traumatised by its earlier experiences and as a result, somewhat psycho-pathological in its orientation. In order to visualise what the face of terrorism is likely to be in the 21st century, it is necessary that we keep following points in mind:

- Terrorism is not aimless. It is driven by various causes.
- Impairment of individual psyche giving it a psycho-pathological skew is what leads persons to become terrorists and NOT race or religion. Despite the 'skew', the terrorist is as rational as a soldier and has normal faculties like logic, discrimination, faith, judgment and so on.
- Terrorists rebuild their self-esteem and violence; and for this, they surrender their individuality to the group, a heavy price indeed.

The various causes which trigger susceptible minds to turn terrorists are discussed below:

- Relative poverty and deprivation of the basic needs of a human being constitute a major reason for the alienation of people from their government. Wherever there are instances of conspicuous consumption being indulged in, adjacent to areas of marginal subsistence, alienation is aggravated. Long periods of neglect towards the problems of the poor and the deprived will motivate many to adopt terrorism as their solution to the problem.
- The prevalence of autocratic and totalitarian regimes in many parts of the world and complete

absence of democracy and suppression of human rights at political, economic and social levels, breeds antagonism and rebellion. This, in turn, gives rise to anti-social radical behaviour and eventually to terrorism.

- There has always been deep suspicion of citizens who do not belong to the majority's racial or religious type. In some cases, this turns to pathological hatred such as Hitler's towards the Jews. This gives rise to 'state terrorism'. In many cases, the reverse phenomenon also takes place, i.e the rise of the minority against the rulers. Such cases of sub-national upsurge become clandestine terrorist movements when confronted by the heavy hand of 'state repression'.
- Corrupt and insensitive governance often triggers violent and sustained adverse reaction. The protests of the 'have nots' can be easily converted by demagogues, radical politicians and some religious fundamentalists into a revolutionary movement, using terrorist methods as its main mode of operation.
- Hatred of the West, specially the USA, is one of the leading causes of terrorism against the USA and Western interests. The birth of this anti-USA feeling can be traced to the period 1948 onwards, till date. It started with the espousal of Israeli's cause by the USA, the spectacular failure of the Arab nations to achieve the level of success that Israel achieved, the defeats that Arab countries suffered in their wars against Israel in 1956, 1967 and even 1983 and, above all, the constant efforts of over-zealous US administrations to 'reform' Arab countries in the mould of the USA – an idea that did not appeal to any Arab country. The USA's self-

defeating efforts earned for them the unqualified hatred of the Arabs. This, coupled with the Cold War period of manipulative diplomacy which the USA practiced, gave rise to the birth of *Al Qaeda* which the former now excoriates as the arch villain of the modern world!

- State terrorism has been alluded to earlier, in connection with Hitler's hatred of the Jews. His aim in eliminating the Jews was to reconstruct German society into a purely 'Aryan' one. Of the same ilk was Chairman Mao Dzedong's Cultural Revolution and his call to 'let a hundred flowers bloom and a hundred schools of thought contend'. No sooner did the flowers bloom, they were ground into the dust as they were 'dangerous revisionist ideas' and the revisionists were sent away to be re-educated! Pol Pot in Cambodia wanted to rebuild a new state on the mass graves of those whom he had sent to death. These instances of state terrorism are caused by the belief that extermination of political threats to totalitarian states will perpetuate their regimes.

We have discussed some of the major causes which terrorists normally espouse – from seeking to change their own government for securing a better life for themselves to attacking regimes which support their enemies; from sub-nationalist urges for separate homelands to state organised 'ethnic cleansing' to 'purify' the society – these are 'causes' that do not appeal to everyone. However, the kind of person we described as being susceptible to becoming a terrorist will find nothing illogical or irrational in these 'causes' and would espouse them faithfully and with zeal. Let us now turn our attention to the face of terrorism in the 21st century – its motivations, weapons, likely outcomes and at the end our examination of these to see how the nations of the world may deal with these violent movements.

The basic observation which we wish to make is that terrorism being a phenomenon born out of the circumstances, hopes and frustrations, desires and hatreds of individual human beings, cannot radically change its contours. Oppressive regimes were to be found in the ancient world even as they are in the modern world. All that has changed is the methodology of repression and the instruments thereof. The terrorist movement which arises as a backlash to that repression, can also only change to the extent of the levels of violence, the weapons and explosives used and the availability of modern communication systems, transportation systems and so on. Having said this, we must hasten to add that terrorism of the 21st century cannot be dealt with in the lackadaisical manner that nations did in the past or in the manner of the cowboys of the Wild West, a' la President Bush. That way, surely, lies disaster. Let us identify what we consider are the major changes that we should expect to see in terrorism today.

The first change that we are likely to encounter is of 'globalisation' of terrorism. Already we find Osama bin Laden (an Arab), sheltering among people of Afghanistan or Pakistan (Afghans or Pathans), working through agents in Europe to strike at targets in the USA, in Africa and elsewhere too. His funding is from a host of international sources and clearly he has the ability to recruit trainee pilots in any corner of the world. In fact, it is not inconceivable that a future 'incarnation' of Osama may run the business of terrorism like a multi-national corporation which, for reasons of security, would need to have a 'legitimate' business as a mainline activity and a 'clandestine' terrorist business as a parallel activity.

It is not unreasonable to expect that rather than start such a corporation *ab initio*, that person may prefer to 'acquire' a running concern which could be adapted for its dual role by and by. We need, therefore, to look on 'globalisation' to hit the terrorist business as well in the coming decade or so – a possible case of fiction anticipating reality.

The second change or development relates to whether the vast number of malcontents in various countries all over the world, would be able to prevail against powerful governments like the USA or the kind of 'coalitions' that the USA rustles up at the slightest provocation. The answer to this is that the 'stand-alone' terrorist groups will not be able to prevail against the USA or USA Inc, as we may call these coalitions of the superpower. To still strike a meaningful blow for their 'cause' with a fair chance of success, these groups will have to approach the new Terror Inc we referred to in the last paragraph. It would be a business arrangement with payments being made either in cash or, more likely, in the form of concessions and privileges being extended to Terror Inc on achieving success. In case they do not wish to avail of the services of Terror Inc, they would still be able to survive but only as harried and hunted fugitives, fleeing from the 'infinite justice' of USA Inc. It would be a poor and graceless existence indeed.

The globalised Terror Inc will also draw the vigorous attention of USA Inc. It is unlikely that the cover provided by their front corporation will last for ever. On the contrary, it is to be expected that the advanced countries of the world will be able to breach the cover in respect of some part, if not the whole of Terror Inc. We expect that this organisation would be aware of the hazards of its occupation and would have taken advance measures to protect its core interests. Measures like using many cover organisations rather than a single, large one, could be one such measure. Terror Inc would then become a modern 'Hydra', like the multi-headed monster of Greek mythology which sprouted two heads for each one cut, off till the great Hercules finally did a remarkable 'cut and cauterise' operation on each neck and its associated head! On their present rather inept showing, neither the USA nor any of its coalition partners seem to have the makings of such a Hercules who can destroy a Hydra-headed Terror Inc.

There is also a distinct possibility that in addition to the basic 'cover' it adopts as a 'shield', Terror Inc will fashion for itself a 'sword' arm consisting of effective measures to 'parry' the thrusts of USA Inc as well as to deliver its own 'riposte' which would seek to paralyse the functioning of its opponents. We visualise a worldwide network of small, clandestine, superbly equipped and trained forces which Terror Inc's clients would organise and raise in their respective areas, under the direction of the HQ of Terror Inc and paid for by them. This clandestine force would react only when activated and remain dormant till then, under various innocuous labels such as Adolf Hitler was adept at inventing. The control of the 'high ground' of cyberspace would be an essential feature of Terror Inc's plans for 'whoever controls the ether will control all modern communications and computer networks' and, through them, everything under the '21st century Sun'. The marvels of modern science and technology can be used by friend and foe alike, the winner in the contest, taking all.

And, finally, the most dreaded possibility that makes many Americans, working on the banks of the Potomac go cold with horror: the Weapons of Mass Destruction (WMD) – the object of US President Bush's fruitless quest in Saddam Hussein's Iraq and now, probably in

Iran; the WMD which led to the ravishment of Iraq though nothing was ever found or even proven with tenable evidence. But superpowers operate under their self-assumed 'divine right' and a country or two bespoiled, is of no account, as long as the search is for WMD – we are merely paraphrasing what the British Prime Minister Blair said in his forgettable defence of the invasion of Iraq before the House of Commons. To revert to the possibility of WMD being acquired by Terror Inc or non-affiliated independent terrorist groups, we believe that the technology and materials to be able to produce nuclear, biological and chemical weapons, are within the reach of any person or organisation determined to acquire them. Fortunately, we have no concrete evidence to the effect that some non-state actors have acquired WMD, but, we cannot deny the possibility that such an event or set of events may have already come to pass. We have the single incident of the 'Sarin' gas attack by the Aum Shinri Kyo group in the Tokyo subway to go by: it blazoned the message that deadly gases are within reach of terrorists. If it happened once, it can happen again. So, we must presume that WMD can become available to terrorists, specially if they unite under Terror Inc. As to whether the atomic bomb or other WMD are likely to be employed by Terror Inc, we can only speculate. The very nature of the atomic bomb should rule out its employment even by terrorist organisations as in the case of nation-states. We believe that there is strength in this assumption. As to other kinds of radiological, chemical and biological weapons, we are not so certain. 'Sarin' was used once; man has used poison gas repeatedly in World War I, Iran-Iraq War and in Vietnam where the USA, today's 'great White Hope', used Agent Orange to destroy Vietnam's flora for a very long time. It could happen again. As to biological weapons, we believe that the paranoia about Anthrax displayed by the USA in the post 9-11 period, indicates that it expected such an attack. Why? Did it supply bio-weapons to Iraq – just as it is reported to have supplied chemical weapons to Iraq for use against Iran though the then President of Iraq, Saddam Hussein, decided to use it against the separatist movement of the Kurds? If so, we can understand why the USA is paranoid about bio-weapons; however, we cannot sympathise with them.

There will be many aspects of 21st century terrorism, which are likely to be not very different from those of the 20th century. Illegal arms trade, the symbiotic relationship between the narcotics trade and arms dealers operating from almost open (but illegal) arms *bazaars,* the use of 'front' shipping companies with their entire fleets owned by terrorists and flying, possibly, a Panamanian or Liberian flag for smuggling weapons and liberal use of bogus 'end user's certificates' to satisfy the legal requirements of arms dealers trading legally – these and many other aspects of 20th century terrorism will remain, and possibly flourish in the 21st century. One aspect which will grow greatly in importance is that of narco-terrorism. With countries the world over coming under pressure to destroy the poppy fields of Asia and the coca plantations of South America, the price of the pernicious end product, heroin or cocaine, will escalate. This will make for increased purchasing power of narcotic drugs in the arms *bazaars* of the world.

Will there be changes in the face of State terrorism – both the Saddam Hussein/Hamas variety and the extreme reaction this provokes from the US Inc, Israel and others? We believe that unless the root causes of terrorism are addressed with sincerity and the breeding grounds of these pathogens cleansed, terrorists and terrorism will always flourish. If our reaction is to 'declare war on terror' as literally as the US Inc is doing now, they may achieve success in killing terrorists but NOT terrorism. Terrorism will flourish as long as we act in the manner of mediaeval 'crusaders' going to chastise the Saracens. It speaks very poorly of the civilizational status of countries which can, even for a moment, regard the mindless killing inflicted on whole populations under the regime of 'War on Terror' as a solution to the human problem that sustains terrorism. The present approach smacks of the 'final solution' when Hitler decided to end the 'Jewish Problem'. We do hope that the US Inc reconsiders its plans for the ongoing 'war'. We hope that lances atilt, like Don Quixote and Sancho Panza, they now do not decide to bring peace and democracy to Iran in the way they did in Iraq. If they do, Bush and Blair are unlikely to be forgiven by history.

Let us return from our excursion into international terrorism into what a vast country like India is likely to suffer at the hands of many varieties of terrorist groups that operate within the country. There are, broadly, home-grown groups and foreign inspired groups. Jammu and Kashmir has both varieties – JKLF, Al Jehad, HUM among the home-grown and JeM, LeT, Al Mansooran among the foreign/foreign inspired groups. Elsewhere in the country, there are leftist extremist groups, religious extremist groups, sub-nationalist/tribal groups. These include MCC, PWG, (CPM-ML), Naxalites (all leftists), Al Umma, Hindu Munnani, Islamic Students' League (all religious), NSCN (both IM and K), ULFA, PLA (all sub-nationalist) and NDFB and BTF (tribal). There are many more groups of each variety but the recitation of their names or histories is not relevant to the present discussion. The point that we wish to make is that India's 'terrorscape' is as varied as India's landscape and seems likely to retain its variety for at least the next decade or two.

Apart from the general observation about the variety of terror groups that we will be finding, the face of terrorism in India is likely to be characterised by the following features:

- Terrorism of all varieties is on the wane in J&K, following sustained pressure from the security forces for over a decade, disillusionment of the people towards terrorism as a route to 'self-determination', disillusionment of the home-grown groups about the chances of success in their fight, the reduction in Pakistan's support to trans-border terrorism following the US pressure and demonstrated Indian resolve to force them to do so, if need be, by going to war against them and above all, the fatigue that people in J&K feel after many years of terrorism and the suffering it has entailed for everyone. Waning terrorism is not likely to die with a mere whimper. On the contrary, we expect that like the sudden blazing of a dying fire, there will be an orgy of terrorist violence before the terrorists either surrender or are killed. These last ditch terrorists are likely to be those from Pakistan or POK and possibly a handful of mercenaries from other Muslim countries. We should expect that these final exhibitions of terrorism in J&K will be directed against soft targets, high visibility infrastructure projects like railways, power plants, communication links and religious places. All nightmares have to end some time and the nightmare of J&K too will end provided the state and the Central Governments decide to wake up and attend to the long-standing problems of the people of the state in an honest, sincere and mission-oriented manner. The administrators must eschew corruption and the police, their inattention to performance of their duties. Above all, the people of J&K must at last speak for themselves and not allow Pakistan or its proxies to take over their fundamental duty towards themselves and the concept of 'Kashmiriat'.

- Leftist extremism will also wane in the foreseeable future, perhaps in as little as a decade, provided the gross economic disparities that are a feature of India's current development profile, are evened out. We believe that the support of leftist political parties to the Union Government will prove to be a catalyst in changing the outlook of the workers and peasants of the leftist movements from a pro-terrorist to a more positive pro-government one. This, together with economic development at a rapid pace, coupled with sincere efforts to remove glaring economic disparities, will help to gradually remove the *raison d'etre* of the leftist extremist groups. This change will be further hastened if India and China achieve greater strategic convergence on various issues and are perceived by our people to be working together for the common good of both peoples. The winds of change are certainly blowing. We should make every effort to see that their momentum is not allowed to drop, as a result of pettiness in politics, ineptness in governance and lack of communication with those who are extremists today out of economic despair. The ball, we must realise, has always been in our court. If we have the national will and our Governments work for it, leftist extremism will soon disappear.
- Religious fundamentalism has entered the Indian political scene in much the same way as a toxin invades the human body and lays it low, maybe, kills it. Whether it is the Hindu outcry against what some Hindus call 'appeasement' of Muslims and denial of the lion's share of living space under the Sun or what some Muslims call discrimination

against them and denial of their place under the Sun, as guaranteed by the Indian Constitution, the resultant clamour created by both groups of fundamentalists, has driven a deep wedge between the communities. The politicians of both groups forget that even if all of them raised their voices to the heavens and voiced their protests, the same Sun will continue to shine, just as it has done since Creation, evenly over all of India, unmindful of who is Hindu or Muslim or of any other religious persuasion! These politicians are doing grave disservice to the country. Unless they rein in their hot headed activist cadres and adopt the language, manner and spirit of a 'single India for all Indians' approach in their politics, the wedge they have driven between communities, is likely to split India and, God forbid, lead to a second partition. We could say much more about the evils of communal politics and how we may escape its worst effects. But aware as we are, of the emotive nature of the subject, all that we will say is that the Indian Army is an object lesson for all of them in communal amity and that our politicians, instead of talking loudly about 'our brave jawans and their defence of the Motherland', should get out to the nearest military units and see how they live, work and play and if necessary, fight for India as Indians, never bothering about who belongs to which religion. Will our politicians, who talk so lovingly about the 'jawan' try to learn the basics of being Indians from them? We entreat them to do so – every one of them. That will rid the ghost of communal strife for ever from our country. The alternative is too grim to contemplate.

- Sub-nationalism and tribalism have given rise to terrorism of a unique type. In the first case, people of India's North-eastern frontier belt, who had been brought under a very tenuous or nominal form of 'control' from Delhi, the capital of the then British India, found the efforts of Free India to bring these people into the national mainstream, irksome. They had come under the influence of Christian missionaries decades ago and the majority of these people were converts to Christianity though vestiges of Animism remained among them. They had also developed a dislike for the people of the plains of Assam and Bengal, whom they regarded as greedy traders and interlopers into their land. For these and many other reasons, their leaders called for the establishment of their own independent homeland. Baulked in its efforts to unify the country and bring these border people into the national mainstream, the Indian Government set about establishing its writ over the area. There was a 'civilised' form of terrorism from the side of the frontier tribesmen and military action from the Government side. This went on for nearly 50 years and now, it seems both sides are keen to settle the matter amicably. There are complicating factors too in the peace process. We are confident that these will be dealt with in a patient and honest manner by all concerned so that the half century long problem of the tribal areas is resolved. As to the problem of sub-nationalism and associated terrorism caused by ULFA and Bodos, there is need for sincerity in politics rather than for military might. Problems caused by illegal immigrants and the threats perceived by tribal people who see their very identity being submerged by the influx, are real problems and cannot be wished away. The concerned leaders of all the interested parties must sit across a table with the state and Central Governments and find an answer to the problems that bedevil Assam. Sincerity must be the watchword in these talks. And against the hostile intelligence agencies that attempt to defeat every peace move, a policy of ruthless elimination should be followed. With this approach, over a period, we should hope to bring down the level of violence in these parts and integrate them into the national mainstream as equal partners in India's march to prosperity and greatness.

The face of terrorism in the 21st century will be as unattractive as it was in the past. With more lethal weapons available to terrorists, it could even turn into a death mask that could bring about the demise of humanity. However, there is no place for pessimism. All nations and the UN should, in their several spheres and on a universal basis, take steps to identify and rectify the causes that led to terrorism in the first place. While 'capping' the existing violence levels, efforts must be made to remove the causes. The mindless cycle of terrorism-counter terrorism-renewed terrorism and so on, must be given up in favour of a more sensible, humane approach. If one follows the principles of sincerity, sympathetic examination of grievances, simultaneity in controlling violence and removal of causes of terrorism and sustained efforts to prevent relapses from occurring, the world can be rid of terrorism in its many forms, in the next two decades or so. We hope, by then, the Bush Doctrine would be only a distant memory.

7

Political Control of the Services

India's armed forces have derived much of their organisational structures and administrative practices from the British who ruled our country for nearly two centuries. Under the British, the Viceroy of India assisted by the Executive Council (like a Cabinet) was in effective charge of all that went on in Britain's largest colony. The Commander-in-Chief, who was, ex officio, the Military Member in the Viceroy's Executive Council, in effect, functioned as the Defence Minister of India and wielded powers, second only to that of the Viceroy. His word was law to colonial India's services with only the Viceroy having the power to alter any direction of the Military Member. The control of the services (initially two and after the raising of RIAF, three) was thus vested in the Executive Council of the Viceroy and exercised by the Military Member. This tradition of control of the services by the political executive ensured that the armed forces remained apolitical and well insulated from the politics of the country, including the freedom movement. Since Independence, the Union Cabinet headed by the Prime Minister, controls all military matters, the Defence Minister being the Executive Head. The line of control that was established in 1950 and is still extant reads: The President (Supreme Commander) – Prime Minister – Defence Minister – Ministers of State / Deputy Ministers in the Defence Ministry – Service Chiefs. The CDS, as and when the Government decides to create the appointment, will rank with the Service Chiefs generally, and on specific matters like handling of Strategic Forces, Andaman Nicobar Command, Medical Services, Defence Perspective Plans, Budget and Defence Intelligence Agency, he will be dealing with the Defence Minister. In addition, he will advise the Government on all Defence matters. The Chairman Chiefs of Staff Committee is currently standing in for the CDS.

The control of the Services in India by the Cabinet is thus, a well established and functioning arrangement and has been instrumental in preserving the apolitical nature of our armed forces, so vital a requirement in genuine democracies.

In this chapter, we shall examine the matter of political control of the services in greater depth, the aberrations that have crept in and what we must do to see that the armed forces are not politicised.

On both the eastern and western flanks of India are countries which, though they inherited virtually the same traditions as we did, saw their armies lose their apolitical character and take upon themselves the governance of their countries. We are clearly referring to Pakistan, Bangladesh and Myanmar (formerly Burma). Despite spells of military rule, Bangladesh is today a democracy under an elected civilian government. However, Pakistan has a military President who is also their Army Chief and a civilian government which does not have freedom of action that all elected governments in genuinely democratic countries have. Their decision can be set aside by the President-cum-Army Chief, should he so desire and the Government itself can be removed by a Chief Executive's fiat. In effect, Pakistan's Government can only be regarded as a government whose freedom of action is decided by the military ruler of the country. Myanmar turned its back on democracy some years ago and is ruled by a military *junta* while the popularly elected leader is not free to take up her democratic mandate. While it is entirely the sovereign right and privilege of any country to decide who shall govern it, we cannot help but state that our experience with democracy has been good and our apolitical armed forces have never attempted to take over the governance of the country.

The phenomenon of the military usurping the authority to govern the country is called 'Praetorianism'. This word is derived from the term 'Praetorian Guards', a body of troops who, in ancient Rome, were charged with the responsibility of protecting the Emperor but, instead, specialised in making and unmaking Emperors. Today, Praetorianism is defined as a situation where the military class of a given society exercises independent power by virtue of an actual or threatened use of force, a 'coup d'etat'. This kind of military intervention in politics is the consequence of the interplay of two sets of factors in a given domestic and external environment. The two factors are:

- The military and its capacity as well as propensity to intervene.
- The society including the socio-political-economic situation and their net effect on the polity.

For a military 'coup' to fructify, both these factors must be mixed optimally, forming a 'critical mass', as it might be said in nuclear science. If the mixture is non-critical, a coup will not materialise.

Let us consider the military factor first. The French Revolution, 1789, established for the first time the concept of 'Sovereignty of the People'. Prior to that climacteric event, rulers derived their mandate to rule, supposedly from Divinity. But the 1789 substitution of 'vox populi' for 'vox Dei' opened up the prospect of generals claiming to represent the people's voice, competing for the right to rule with those who once exercised that power through Divine right. France settled the matter energetically. The Royalty was slaughtered and a military man, Napoleon Bonaparte, became the Emperor of France. This set the precedent for the military to rise against the 'Ruler' or 'Government' to safeguard the 'Nation'.

Thus, two major conclusions emerged from the French Revolution: first, the voice of the people is all-powerful and second, the military could overthrow the 'Ruler' or 'Government' legitimately if it was acting in accordance with the voice of the people. The second consequence was fraught with danger for all rulers and governments as the military could invoke the voice of the people and overthrow them. To stave off this, the rulers in Europe began to professionalise their armies. This, they sought to do by building into the ethos of the military, the concept of the soldier regarding the ruler as his 'client' and, no matter who the 'client' was, the soldier would fight – not so much for 'him', but because it was his profession to fight for a client – any client. This idea is today called 'supremacy of the civil over the military' and seeks to keep the military out of politics. Obviously, in some newly independent countries in which the freedom movement was led by the military, the concept of civil supremacy did not 'take' or was very difficult to apply.

A few words on the capacity of the military to intervene in politics, will not be out of place. The military has tremendous advantages over civilian organisations. It has a highly centralised command structure, a clearly defined hierarchy, discipline of the highest order, excellent tele-communication network, high mobility and a monopoly of heavy weaponry. As defenders of the nation's frontiers, the military is held in high esteem by the people and the countless monuments as tribute to the 'Unknown Soldier' in virtually every country in the world, are held in sentimental veneration by the people. So, the military has great potential to succeed, should it wish to intervene in politics. It also has the intangible but priceless asset of 'esprit de corps' which welds it into a homogenous force of great power, virtually irresistible, if it should decide to intervene in politics.

There are a few 'negatives' that reduce somewhat the power of the military in the 'intervention' mode. Firstly, the bulk of its colossal firepower is unusable. In any case, only very small forces are generally required to undertake a coup. Secondly, the military has its own imperfections like the gap between officers and enlisted men, ethnic or regional composition of the forces and the curious phenomenon of coups often generating further coups, like it happened in Argentina, Columbia, Venezuela, Syria, Iraq and so on.

What could motivate the military to intervene in politics? We can do no better than list the five motivations identified by S.E. Finer in his masterly treatise, '*Comparative Government*'. These are:

- Concern for national interest, whether true or only claimed. Pakistan Army is often motivated to intervene in national interest.
- Class interest, specially if the military caste is from middle-class background as opposed to the rich land-owners and 'sahibs' who may be the governing class.

- Particularist interest, which may be regional, ethnic, communal or even linguistic. Africa is full of such 'particularist' influences which have caused countless civil wars and coups.
- Corporate self-interest of the military, a very important factor where the military perceives a threat to its place in the country if its budgets are cut frequently, its political influence curbed, 'rival' armed police or militia forces are formed and so on.
- Personal interest can also be an important motivating factor.

These five motivations given by Finer, mathematically form 31 combinations, any one of which can cause a coup. Not surprisingly, few coups display identical motivations.

Let us now leave the military factor and go on to the social factor. The societal conditions which favour military intervention in politics are:

- Level of political culture: Finer classifies political culture in ascending order as minimal, low, developed and mature. The lower the political culture, the more coup-prone those countries will be.
- Provision for constitutional change of government inhibits coups whereas, non-provision or non-workable provisions, favour coups.
- Economic development, specially industrialisation, diminishes the propensity of the military to intervene. Poverty, disease, illiteracy, high birth/death rates, endemic hunger/starvation and extreme disparities in the distribution of wealth are frequent causes for coups. However, even a

healthy economy which may have become crisis-ridden due to a variety of factors (large-scale unemployment, runaway inflation, a 'bad' war, major defeat, chronic political instability, etc.) could also lead to coups as happened in the case of Argentina and Brazil.

- Foreign influence, especially foreign military aid, has a tendency to erode national political independence as was seen repeatedly in some of the countries of Latin America. This could give rise to military intervention, specially in countries with minimal or low political culture.
- Civilian control of the military is a bulwark against its intervention if the control has been institutionalised in an enlightened and not arbitrary manner. If the control is perceived as arbitrary, even highly professional officer corps like in the German, French or Pakistani armies could turn Praetorian, thus defeating the very aim of civilian control.

There are also a few environmental factors which favour military intervention in politics. These include:

- Low domestic morale due to poor socio-economic or socio-political conditions.
- Weak public opinion.
- External interference in domestic affairs.
- Occurrence of coups in the region/neighbourhood.
- Support given to coup leaders from abroad.

The excursion into the realm of Political Theory was for the purpose of underscoring the rationale for political control of the military, its genesis and the conditions under which military intervention in politics could take place.

Let us now examine how successful political control of the military has been in India, some instances of 'excessive' control or even interference by politicians, in purely professional military/domestic matters and what we as a nation need to do about it.

At the outset, let us congratulate ourselves that though we may have frittered away some of the valuable legacies of the British Raj, political control over the military is not one of them. It has withstood the test of 58 years of freedom, many changes of Government, the rise and fall of political leaders and parties at the helm of affairs, wars, internal unrest, communal riots, economic depression (and now a vibrant, rapidly growing economy) and a swelling of our population from under 400 million to over one billion. To survive under such varied and challenging conditions, it is clear that the principle of Political Control over the military must be sound, responsive to the country's needs and fully acceptable to our political and military establishments. The credit for this must go to both the political and the military classes, the former for their enlightened approach and the latter for their discipline and abiding commitment to national interest. Having said this, let us also admit that it has not been smooth sailing all the way. There have been instances of aberrant behaviour from both the political and the military classes. There have also been individual acts of commission and omission at variance with the concept of either civil supremacy or the professional autonomy of the military. We will examine these to the extent necessary to enable us to draw useful lessons and guidance for the future.

Issues Relating to Policy

Even after Independence, India's political leaders found it convenient to keep the Army, Navy and the Air

Force out of the 'policy' making bodies. The services HQ were left at the level that the British left them – that of being 'attached offices' of the Ministry of Defence. Even at the level of the Defence Minister and Service Chiefs, exchanges on major matters of Defence policy were few and far between, the Defence Minister's weekly meetings with the Service Chiefs being used to update the Minister and equip him to negotiate questions in Parliament. Often, these meetings were deferred, as 'more important' activities claimed the time of the Minister. All Ministers were not inclined to treat their weekly meetings with the Service Chiefs as lightly as this. Many of them would hold regular meetings at which very meaningful discussions about all Service matters including policy matters took place, giving the Services a sense of participation in policy formulation and much greater involvement in implementing such polices. The result of the 'attached office' status taken together with periodic lack of interest in Service matters from the Defence Minister, was the greater role and authority assumed by the Defence bureaucracy. The Defence Secretary, with his nearness to the Defence Minister, often began to exercise power on the Minister's behalf and was, quite often, regarded as the de facto Defence Minister. The 'supremacy of the civil over the military' was thus effectively changed from the supremacy of the political authority to that of the civilian bureaucracy. We must be fair and state that not all Defence Secretaries and their subordinates assumed such false colours. Some, who were overbearing, impatient and a touch too grandiose in their thinking did and this soured Service HQ-Ministry of Defence relations. In fact, readers may recall, how a tabloid magazine published a photo-copy of a representation, jointly signed by the three Chiefs, to the Defence Minister, seeking the removal of the Defence Secretary as they had no confidence in him. What a ghastly state of affairs! Such a thing could never have happened if ministerial responsibilities had been fulfilled more appropriately and bureaucratic egos not allowed to bloat to such unhealthy levels. Service Chiefs too, who allowed such a state of affairs to arise, must be regarded as blameworthy for they did not act in time and allowed the whole unsavoury matter to come into the public domain instead of nipping it in the bud.

A word here about Defence Ministers. There must always be a Defence Minister of Cabinet rank. The practice of the Prime Minister holding the Defence portfolio, is fraught with many negative possibilities. He will not be able to give the attention to Defence that it deserves. The Minister of State who he may be relying on to discharge his duties as the Head of the Ministry, may not be of the requisite calibre and be inclined to cede his authority to the bureaucrats while he enjoys the full perks and privileges that are considered a part of the ministerial appointment. No ministry can be run in this casual manner, least of all the Ministry of Defence. This point has been highlighted as what has happened before, can happen again. It should not, if the country's interests are to be safeguarded.

On the subject of Defence Ministers, we feel that with coalition governments, having now become the norm and their longevity being unpredictable, it is necessary to appoint as Defence Minister, a person who is mature, well-respected, has had experience of military service or, has become known for his deep interest in and study of defence matters or, may have served in the Ministry of Defence in a junior capacity with distinction. The appointee should be even tempered, receptive to the views of others, keen to learn, decisive, capable of sustained hard work over a prolonged period, sympathetic to the rank and file, impartial, honest and sincere in his stewardship of the ministry. Above all, he should be imbued with two attributes in abundant measure – common sense and a sense of humour. Such a paragon of virtue may rarely be found. The one who comes closest to our 'wish list' would be the right choice for appointment as Defence Minister. Likewise, other ministers placed under him should be similarly selected. This will contribute immensely to efficiency and smoothness in the functioning of the Ministry of Defence.

While we are on the subject of political aberrations/ failure, we would like to point out that members of the Defence Consultative Committee of the Parliament can and should improve their overall approach to Defence matters. Their role is a very important one. Watching over the country's interests in a key area is a very demanding task and calls for special exertions from the MPs in the committee. If, instead of their party affiliations, they are inspired by genuine zeal to understand and contribute to the better conduct of Defence affairs, they would have earned the country's gratitude.

The political aberration of Services HQ being 'attached offices' or mere appendages without any role in policy making, has been corrected with the formation of the Integrated Defence Staff with personnel from the three services and the bureaucracy staffing it – at least, in theory. With the 'headless wonder' – i.e the Integrated Defence Staff still to find its feet after over three years of existence, an early review of what has been achieved so far, is essential in order to remove impediments in its realising its chartered aims. Perhaps the manner of integration is faulty. By allowing each Service to retain its identity in the organisation tree and the civilian wings of the Government doing likewise, we appear to have achieved only a thin veneer of integration. This needs early attention. Perhaps, the sanctioning of the post of Chief of Defence Staff and connected appointments, would be a corrective action. Further delay in the matter will make the entire exercise of Defence Staff integration meaningless.

We must commend one practice which seems to have started in the past few years, – the practice of inviting the Service Chiefs to attend meetings of the Cabinet Committee on Security where national security issues are to be discussed. There was provision for such invitations being extended even earlier, but it was used only in exceptional cases. The current practice enables the Service Chiefs to fully contribute on national security matters and enables the Cabinet Committee on Security to arrive at better conclusions/decisions. This practice should be formally institutionalised.

On operational matters, there is a definite need to meticulously record the proceedings of various meetings, Councils of War and the like, so that the rationale for any action taken at a critical period in our history, does not become a matter for speculation but can be read easily from the records. It is even more important that Government's directives to the Chairman, Chiefs of Staff Committee, and to the Service Chiefs, invariably be in writing. There is an inherent ring of confidence about a Government directive in writing, which verbal directives lack, being amenable to flexible interpretation. In matters of war and peace, every functionary and every organ of the state has the right to receive formal orders and directives, so that what is intended to be done is not only done properly, but also done with the awareness that those who issued those orders/directives have done so after conclusive deliberations. It speaks highly of the relationship of mutual trust that has developed between the Service Chiefs and the leadership that the Chiefs have unquestioningly implemented their leader's directions even when these were issued verbally. But times change, personalities change and trust may, sadly, 'wither on the vine'. We owe it to history and to our nation that the leaders record their decisions with reasons and issue their directives/orders in writing.

These were some of the major areas at the national political level where there is room for doing things differently. There will be, no doubt, some differences of opinion from the author's views. This is also desirable as debate and discussion enable one to look at a problem in its entirety from many angles so that the resulting conclusions may be logical and sound.

Non-Policy Issues

We have in India, the world's largest, genuine democracy. Our independent nationhood took birth in 1947, a mere 58 years ago. We have shaken off the effects of colonial rule and lack of infrastructure for development, and are, today, the fourth largest economy in the world. Our future is bright and we are heading energetically towards a high level of prosperity. But in many ways, we have not done well. Our levels of corruption are among the highest in the world. The level of probity in public affairs and commerce, are considered by many to be low. Society in India has steep gradients between the rich and the poor. What is worse, the bonds of compassion and fellow-feeling are almost non-existent between the two. But India is one nation and it is from this nation that we recruit personnel for our armed forces and elect our political leaders. Politicians and servicemen belong to the same slice of India's society. The defining difference between the two is military training. We shall leave this thought hanging as a backdrop, to what we have to say in the ensuing paragraphs.

While claiming no superhuman attributes for the Indian serviceman, be he an officer or enlisted man, it will not be an exaggeration if we say that he is generally very honest, straightforward in his dealings, has a well developed sense of right and wrong and a very high sense of honour – the honour of his regiment, family, state and country. These attributes keep him generally on the right path so that the Indian soldiery is regarded very highly throughout the world. Yet, we find courts martial taking place every now and then, lurid reports appear in the papers of how a soldier ran amok and killed six others or how a group of soldiers were involved in an affray in a public place. Closer examination of the circumstances of some of these acts of indiscipline may reveal startling facts. Without making any attempt to absolve the soldiers of their offences, we need to study the reasons why a trained and disciplined soldier 'goes off the rails'. Clearly, there could be reasons which are concerned with his military service and others which arise out of his interactions with the outside world, be it the revenue officers in his native district, the functionaries of the Indian Railways, civilian doctors and other professionals he may have had to deal with. The soldier who goes home from field area service, perhaps twice a year, finds many differences from the life in the military. Some of these differences are:

- Complaints are not attended to by revenue officials in the chain. Sometimes, even an august personage like the Deputy Commissioner or Collector of his District ('Mai Baap' to the people) is unresponsive to his problems. He is disillusioned and frustrated.
- The professionals he approaches for various forms of assistance are often patronising and quite a few demand illegal gratification for what clearly is their duty to do, gratis. He gets even more frustrated.

- Traders are out to make quick profits and do this by overcharging, underweighing, adulterating and on occasion, selling at exhorbitant prices after hoarding stocks to create an artificial scarcity. The soldier is bewildered.
- His approach to the Member of the Legislative Assembly from his constituency is a nightmare as he had to grease many palms before he could even see the great man and when he did, the great man stated that he could not help him because our soldier belonged to a certain caste! He is shocked.
- He tells his aged mother and young wife about all that befell him when he took up their problems. They told him, "Nobody listens to those who need help". The soldier is enraged at the thought that his folks are "helpless".
- And if it is election time, the soldier sees the aspiring candidates from his constituency visit his house and with folded hands to seek his precious vote! The soldier is too well mannered to say anything nasty to a visitor to his home. But he is disgusted.

The cumulative effect of his interaction with the society to which he too belongs was, to say the least, destabilising on the mind of the soldier. Could there be greater disservice to the country by its citizens, than when they force a soldier who guards their life and liberty, to entreat, cajole, bribe and threaten people to get the welfare of his family attended to? And as for the legislator who values caste more than his duty to his constituency, it would have been better if he had not been elected. This synthetic, composite example illustrates the usual grievance of a soldier: "Nobody listens to me. Everyone wants a *quid pro quo* for doing his job. And even my MLA for whom I voted, finds that

I am too low born to be helped"! As we said before, this story is apochryphical. It has been put in, so as to illustrate what a soldier faces when he goes home and seeks a better dispensation for him from his countrymen – politicians, bureaucrats, professionals and others. The politician is the person who should take the lead in the matter, even as he did when canvassing support for his election; hence this story. Are our politicians doing enough for our soldiers?

But the same politician is quite active while approaching military authorities on behalf of his soldier kinfolk and friends with a variety of requests. The requests range from seeking a suitable posting to a plum appointment, cancellation of posting to a 'difficult' area, extension of posting at a place beyond the normal tenure, leave, regularisation of period of overstayal of leave, pardon for an offence, attempt to avoid courts martial by using political influence, reinstatement of discharged persons, seeking discharge of persons prematurely, getting a job in defence establishments, being recruited and so on. While the military authorities accommodate such requests as are valid, the use of the MP's or Minister's letterhead, calculated to overawe the recipient and achieve an unauthorised favour for one of his kinfolk, is a ploy all too frequently used. The simple soldier is taken 'for a ride' by his political representative and while the latter's purpose is served, the former loses some of his confidence in and respect for the political class. More importantly, he drops a notch or two in his own eyes for having granted an unauthorised favour to a politician's kin. Not all military officers react like this. Quite a few tell the MLA or MP that what they request for, is not permitted under the rules. But some do and they encourage the political class to keep making unauthorised demands on the military. This is often the starting point of politicisation of the Army.

The politically 'infected' officer will seek his 'quid pro quo' at some time or the other and will try to use his new found political influence for the achievement of his own aims – perhaps a choice posting, a foreign course and, as so often happens, a promotion into or in the selection grade which had been turned down by the Selection Board. Sadly, such cases are not infrequent. Often, the politician who peddles his influence for an undeserving officer in this manner, is doing this as an 'investment' in his own interest. Perhaps, the beneficiary officer will be able to serve him in good stead one day. Such political influence peddling is not only pernicious as it is an immoral act, it is also a grave disservice to the discipline of the military and the apolitical nature of the Services. This is how politicisation starts at the grassroots level of the Services. At this level, we may treat both the politician and the serviceman as blameworthy, each in his own way.

There is the 'senior league' corruption of the serviceman, usually a middle or senior level officer, for which the seasoned and successful politician who has an axe to grind, is to be fully blamed. The military officer, in such cases, is often an unwary victim of the politician's intentions. It usually starts at some social or private venue where the officer, attending the function in his personal capacity, is introduced to the politician as a 'rising star', the man to watch etc., and to cap it all, his caste or home district or parentage is made known to the politician. The latter notes the details of the officer and sets about deliberately cultivating him for whatever use he has in mind for him. The officer too, pleased that a 'big' man from his native place or community or whatever, is recognising him as a person of high potential, is happy to go along with the politician. This kind of an acquaintance develops to a stage when the politician goes out of his way to 'help out' the officer in his career or uses his political clout to get him out of a problem, so that the officer starts feeling beholden to the politician. It is at this stage that the 'quid pro quo' begins to be exacted, imperceptibly gently at first, but, as time goes on, increasingly more peremptorily. We cannot spell out what precisely the politician's pound of flesh might be – it could be lucrative contracts for a kinsman; it could be placement of orders for some item which he or someone he is interested in, is producing; or something else of that nature which involves bending the rules or 'looking the other way' or whatever. The officer is trapped. The unholy association continues thereafter till the politician finds that there is no more to be gained from it and 'drops' the officer from his invitees' list. The military, thereafter, have to 'carry' a politically 'experienced' officer or as we prefer to call him, 'politically infected' officer. Such officers have seldom been known for harmonising with their colleagues or, keeping away from politicians and politics, where they once burnt their fingers. They are liabilities to the military.

Another class of politically sensitised serviceman is one who comes from a political background. We have, in the pages of history of independent India, more than one political family, whose scions have served in the armed forces and reverted to politics. Some of these families have a long history of having been the ruling families of India's erstwhile princely states. Their approach to soldiering and politics has been of 'one piece' if one might so describe it. They retain within themselves, a healthy respect for the apolitical nature of the military and have never sought to bring politics into the services. Likewise, those who have served in the military and changed to politics, have never tried to 'use' the military as a stepping stone in their political careers. We have to admit that there have been many erstwhile princes and maharajas who have been exemplars of propriety when they were with the Army and who, when they left it, conducted themselves with dignity and without capitalising on their exposure to the Army. We are aghast at how the 'nouveau political princes' conduct themselves if they were lucky enough to have had an armed forces exposure. They have much to learn about the armed forces before they realise the harm their actions have caused to them.

Politicisation of the military is a self-defeating exercise in a democracy. We pointed out earlier that Praetorianism raises its ugly head under certain socio-economic-political conditions. In India, we are fortunate that the wisdom of the founding fathers has made Praetorianism virtually impossible. However, it has not insulated the country from rampant politicians who seek to achieve their ends through any means whatever, and to whom the man in uniform, is yet another person to do his bidding. We are apprehensive that the greed for the 'fish and loaves' of office, may not lead to a politician corrupting the military establishment and wrenching it from its age-old moorings of loyalty, apolitical nature and the concept of Service before Self.

We would recommend that the sort of military discipline we imbibed through our formative years and which stood us in very good stead, be made available to our fellow citizens. We would like to see our countrymen at large, sharing this great blessing. Over 70 percent of India's population is below the age of 35 years. It is indeed a mind-bogglingly young country that we inhabit. If this 70 per cent youth of our population could be schooled in the virtues of discipline and being true to the oath of loyalty to the country, then we have the immediate possibility of this vast youthful nation, taking giant strides on the route to becoming the greatest nation on planet Earth. We feel that the National Cadet Corps movement be given much greater emphasis and attention. We also recommend strongly that every Government servant or anyone who is serving in a Government assisted organisation, educational institution *et al,* should be required to undergo Territorial Army training for two months every year, for the first four years of his service so that he imbibes soldierly qualities and learns the virtues of discipline at first hand. They should also be allowed a Territorial Army liability for a further period of three years, should they so desire.

As to our politicians, we have nothing against them except that we, as a nation, have transited from being colonials to being, nominally, the greatest democracy on Earth, without adequate preparation. We find that the spirit of sacrifice and service of the Gandhian era has vaporised. We see that politics which was once a service has now become an occupation, a profession. We seem to have lost the faith we had in honest toil and 'service without expectations', as the 'Gita' enjoins on us. And above all, we seem to have supplanted our entire pantheon of gods with just one: Money or Power. Unfortunately, our political class seems to have become fixated on 'Power' to the exclusion of all else. Perhaps a good dose of old fashioned 'discipline' will do them a world of good. We would strongly recommend that no person who aspires to contest an election for MLA or MP be allowed to do so unless he has undergone training as an NCC cadet for a period of three years with high attendance, or alternatively, carried out TA training for two months each year, for three years. The aim is to make them think more for their country than for their party or themselves – a sad fixation that seems to be the ruling characteristic of the political class today.

We are aware that we have moved from the captioned subject imperceptibly to the subject of what ails our political class today. That *was* the intention. We have suggested certain remedies to lift our youth and political class from the indifferent levels where they are today, to one that will make them a credit to a new India. We hope that our words will provoke thought among right thinking Indians so that the world's most youthful nation may also become the world's most disciplined and progressive one. The mere thought of 700 million young Indians, all disciplined, all patriotic and all with a high sense of self-belief, marching together, is awe-inspiring. It need not be a militaristic image. It could be what we believe is India's true métier – spiritual and moral exemplars for the world, strong and yet benignly disposed towards others; prosperous and generous with her aid, guarding her possessions but never coveting another's, with mastery of the arts and sciences and using these for the good of all. It is such an India that should be the goal of every young Indian – each one of the 700 million people that we spoke of. If they set their sights high on the achievable goal of fashioning such an India as we have envisioned, the 21st century may well mark the dawn of a happier, better age.

And as to politicians who would lead the military and gullible citizens astray, they should be able to foresee their end in the beginning of our 'new India'.

8

Foreign Policy and National Security

The 20th century saw the world polarised between two Power Blocs – the USA and its Allies and the Soviet Union and its Allies – with a large number of countries of the Third World, not aligned to either of them. India was one of the founder-leaders of this Non-aligned Group of Nations with the then Prime Minister of India, Mr. Jawaharlal Nehru being regarded universally as the chief architect of the Non-aligned movement along with Marshal Tito of Yugoslavia and President Nasser of Egypt. The leading lights of this movement have all passed into history, and so have the Soviet Union and its Bloc, as of 1990. There then arose a situation, wherein the Non-aligned Nations had to reconsider their relationship with the remaining superpower, the USA, or decide to remain with the non-aligned Movement whose *raison d'etre* had largely vanished. The last decade of the 20th century, presented these nations with this dilemma.

That decade also saw the process of globalisation of the world economy gather momentum rapidly. New regimes of trade and tariffs, economic liberalisation,

WTO and formation of mega-trading-blocs were the buzzwords of that period. India too had awakened from its slumber and instituted far-reaching economic reforms to put the country on an accelerated growth path. This process, set in motion some 15 years ago, is continuing. With the complete attention on economic transformation, our external relations did not receive as much attention as they might have otherwise done, except with our neighbour and adversary, Pakistan. We had not grown out of the habit of looking at the world through the prism of Pakistan distorting our view and, in fact, even today, we are not entirely free of this morbid fixation on Pakistan. However, the Gulf War of 1991, when the USA and its allies took Iraq to task for the invasion of Kuwait and its subsequent slow strangulation of that hapless country with, sadly, the acquiescence of the UN, made us aware of a major qualitative change in the attitude of the USA towards the rest of the world generally and the smaller countries in particular. The new USA was quite different from the one which launched the Marshal Plan for post-war reconstruction or, which under Public Law 480, made liberal food aid available to India among others. This was a more authoritarian, self-centred and self-serving USA that the world saw from about 1990 onwards. Perhaps, having seen its only opponent collapse, the USA found the leadership of the world presented to it and had seized it with both hands, fully determined that nothing will be allowed to come between it and its unchallenged dominance of the world – not the UN, not international laws or treaties, not morals or ethics and not even the opinion of its own fair-minded people. A new 'empire' had come into being, the Empire of the USA.

India flirted with the idea of fostering a closer relationship with the USA and despite the sanctions imposed on it after the Pokharan nuclear tests, by and large, India continued working in that direction. The motive was to leverage maximum advantage from the USA in its adversarial relationship with Pakistan, a relationship that became abyssmal after Pakistan's aggression in the Kargil sector in 1999. These efforts did yield some results for a while as Pakistan, for some time, had to suffer some studied gestures of US' displeasure and was 'talked down' to by the US officials a number of times in their keenness to assure India that they were 'pressurising' Pakistan to stop trans-border terrorism against India. There was really nothing achieved beyond comforting US assurances – the traditional 'tea and sympathy'. Pakistan managed to mollify the USA by 'apparent' compliance with its demands, subterfuge and plain falsehoods. India watched all this in dismay. And then Osama bin Laden struck at the World Trade Centre, New York and the Pentagon, Washington DC. Those terrible acts of terrorism on 11th September, 2001, changed forever how the USA would view the rest of the world.

Stung by having been attacked at home in this dastardly manner, outraged at the grievous loss of life and by the blow to its pride that the attacks against the symbols of national power represented, the US Government reacted with ferocity. President George W. Bush proclaimed war on international terrorism. He and his administration were quick to tell the world that the 'arch-villain' Osama bin Laden, who masterminded the 9-11 attacks, was being sheltered by the 'evil' Taliban rulers of Afghanistan. So Bush ordered attacks on Afghanistan. He was at his persuasive best in drumming up support for his war on terror. He thundered, 'If you are not with us, you are against us'! And so, Afghanistan was reduced to rubble, the Taliban were duly ousted and Karzai was installed as the President at Kabul. In all these actions, Pakistan was a 'front line state', which, despite having been the chief patron of the Taliban regime, threw open its land, air space, airfield facilities, the services of the 'redoubtable' ISI and even its ground troops to the Americans in their War on Terror. India watched all this with a sense of frustration. Even its 'get tough with Pakistan' policy, enunciated after the abortive 13th December, 2001, attack on the Indian Parliament was stymied, as the Americans believed that any action against Pakistan by India would reduce the ability of the former to assist them in their war. So they promised us that they would restrain Pakistan from indulging in cross-border terrorism against India, so that they could use its support in their War on Terror against Afghanistan! And we believed them! Though we had our armed forces ready to fight India's war against Pakistan-inspired terror against us, we let the USA's war have priority. The Nawabs of Lucknow could not have been more accommodating!

The year 2002 passed. Pakistan, though it had been initially reluctant to alienate its own Muslim population by aiding the Americans in their war against the ultra-orthodox Muslim Taliban regime in Afghanistan, had by now whole-heartedly thrown in its lot with the USA-led alliance. After all, states teetering on the brink of 'failure' and dictators skating on thin ice have to adopt such survival techniques as are taught in the Special Services Group Training Centre of Pakistan. In 2004, the USA after offering India the 'moon' in terms of 'strategic partnership' and partial lifting of sanctions, proclaimed Pakistan's new status as 'Major Non-NATO Ally'. Pakistan would receive enhanced military material, training and advice under this new appellation – perhaps even receive F-16 aircraft, which our neighbour has set its heart on, even though there are better aircraft available in the markets of the world (it must be the monetary concession to a major non-NATO ally). Be that as it may, India's overtures to befriend the USA in a far more meaningful relationship have not even 'got to first base' to use an American phrase. We are where we were; getting 'tea and sympathy', a few 'Firefinder' radars and vague offers of F-16s, perhaps F-18s, P3C Orion etc., at the Bangalore Air Show 2005. And Strobe Talbott, with whom our own Jaswant Singh had long and 'important' discussions under the Clinton regime, was back here in India recently to say that we are the real allies in the War on Terrorism. That perhaps is a sample of, 2005 brand of humour.....

We believe that we have allowed the USA to use us in whatever manner it wanted. The USA did the same with Pakistan. But Pakistan has got something for it: absolution for its sins, money to pay interest on its debts, arms in the pipeline and above all, the reassurance that India "can go to the rooftops and cry but you'll always be our pet!" That is the extent of success achieved by our foreign policy experts in two successive regimes. It seems a pity to waste any more time on them.

What are India's interests in foreign policy matters? That, we believe, should be the starting point of our quest for a credible foreign policy vis-à-vis the USA. India's primary interest in foreign policy is to ensure for herself freedom to decide, act and progress without curtailing a similar right of any other nation to do so. We are nobody's vassals. We aim to live in amity and friendship with every neighbour and with all else in the world. We aim to secure for ourselves allies who will be a source of support and strength to us in all difficulties including war that may befall us. And we expect that our foreign policy will enable our country to get a long and unbroken period of peace, so that we may overcome the effect of years of exploitation and neglect and raise India to a level of prosperity, unrivalled in its long and glorious history. The 'mandarins' of South Block may well have many other aims but we hope and pray that rank opportunism and 'kowtowing' before a powerful country for temporary gains are not part of these.

If we agree that these should be our interests from the foreign policy point of view, then how do we take forward our relationship with the USA? Our starting point has to be that we cannot ignore a country as strong as the USA. The Country will, therefore, watch with great interest, the outcome of Prime Minister Manmohan Singh's visit to the USA in July 2005. It should be our endeavour to engage with the USA *on terms of strict parity* in all matters on which *we choose to engage with them,* such as commerce and trade, science and technology, tourism and travel, medicine, health and adventure sports.

We cannot, however, understand why our leaders should not have vehemently rejected the US Secretary of State, Condoleezza Rice's fairly plain 'hint' to us, in March 2005, that the USA would not like to see the Iran-India oil pipeline project to be finalised as the USA has misgivings about Iran. And our repeated flirtation with the idea of buying American war planes under very 'attractive' terms including licenced production in India despite the USA's poor track record with us in defence deals, appears to be most shortsighted, if not worse. India need not overly concern itself if 'X' or 'Y' aircraft manufacturer in the USA is forced to lay off 5000 persons if their 'order book' is not replenished quickly, such as by an order for 126 F-16 Falcons or F-18 Hornets. That is Mr. Bush's problem. We should concern ourselves solely with our nation's security interests, and making the USA a major defence supplier to us, is certainly not in our interest.

There is no sense in doing more in military-to-military relations than exchange visits, courses, sports teams and very controlled intelligence exchanges on matters not relating to our friends. In other words, we believe that we have to go back in time, to say 1997-98 or so, to regain our self-respect as a nation, something we lost in the eyes of most of our countrymen when in their Metternich like zeal, our leaders dragged us into positions where we were obliged to do the bidding of a far more powerful country. We believe that while we build up our strength to a level adequate to deter any thought of misadventure against us by anyone including the superpower, we should forge such alliances and treaties as will link us with countries in roughly the same situation as we are, in a mutual aid and security framework which will discourage any nation including the USA from dictating to us or meddling in our internal or external affairs. Such an arrangement should not be, in any way, objectionable to any other country, as it will have no mandate for military action except in a defensive mode and that too after detailed mutual consultations and arousal of the UN Security Council. A security arrangement of this nature would include Russia, China and India.

Russia has been our tried and trusted friend for over 55 years. It has inherited over 60 percent of the assets of the USSR and is a member of the G-8 Group of rich countries. It has ample natural resources like half of the world's gas, a third of the world's oil, huge hydro-electric potential, high grade coal deposits, gold, iron ore etc, vast areas of virgin land and well-trained and hardy manpower. The Russian Federation was in a state of decline following the collapse of the USSR, till 1996-97 when it started registering a positive growth rate again. The country is well led, politically stable and though it suffers from a variety of 'drag' factors like corruption, organised crime and unemployment, it is very firmly on the path to socio-economic and socio-political recovery. Our relations with the Russian Federation are already well established. Strategic cooperation, defence cooperation including joint manufacture of supersonic cruise missiles, economic linkages in the form of investments, trade and joint ventures and a fair level of people-to-people contacts, all indicate that Russo-Indian friendship is bound to grow. The fact that China and Russia have mended their once strained relations and forged strong economic and political linkages over the past five years or so, augurs well for a triangular security arrangement involving Russia, China and India.

There were many eyebrows that were raised when we mooted such an idea in 2003 (*'The Writing on the Wall : India Takes on the USA, 2017'* by this author). There were many who talked of unsettled Sino-Indian borders leading to claims and counter-claims, likelihood of economic rivalry for the 'numero uno' position in Asia, initially and later on, in an even wider arena and so on. Some political scientists of the USA have widely publicised their view that because of their history of geo-political primacy, China may adopt an assertive grand strategy once it judges that it has fully developed its national strength. These experts postulate that China will be hegemonistic and come into conflict with the USA, already an acknowledged hegemon! To hold a resurgent China in check, they offer preemptive containment of China (incorporating India among others in the containment 'wall'), prevention of China acquiring such capabilities, as could threaten the US interests anywhere in the world and if need be, diplomatic and economic sanctions against it. Should this array of policy options fail, they are prepared to recommend military measures to check China.

We differ with these political scientists on two counts:

- There has been a sea change in attitude of the Chinese towards the rest of the world as is evident from their track record since the Japanese invasion of China in the last century. Far from displaying any return to hegemonistic ambitions, the Chinese have set their face firmly against hegemony in any form, be it the Japanese hegemony, Soviet hegemony and now the hegemony of the USA. It seems extremely unlikely that having been conditioned for over 70 years to abhor hegemony, they would practice it themselves. Our belief is that the only hegemon the world has today – i.e the USA, will lose its primacy not due to Chinese actions but more because of the universal hatred its policies are beginning to inspire among the nations of the world. So it was with the Romans, so it was with the Ottomans too; and so it seems it shall be with the sole superpower and hegemon, the USA.

- Our second objection to the theory of the US political scientists is that China is perhaps one of the most pragmatic and hard-headed nations of the world. Having overcome innumerable challenges, it became free in 1950 and over the last 55 years, China has worked single-mindedly to shake off the legacy of its colonial past and to achieve for its people, a decent standard of living. China has taken in its stride the wave of economic liberalisation and globalisation, and without losing any of its enthusiasm for the philosophy of Marx and Mao Zedong, it has wrought the miracle of turning Shanghai into a metropolis to rival Tokyo or New York. Will China risk its indubitable economic prosperity on counter-productive assertiveness or will it try to improve upon its achievements by bringing in better income distribution and regional parity within the country? We believe China will not be assertive in the manner envisaged by the political scientists of the West.

Some of our Indian 'eye-brow-raisers' speak of a Sino-Indian rivalry for primacy in Asia and later in the world. The idea is a non-starter. As of now, India may catch up with the Chinese, in terms of economic prosperity and military strength, in about 20 to 30 years, provided we carry out the much needed internal political and administrative corrections early. As of now, we have no spare economic, military or political capacity to challenge China for the leadership of Asia. In any case, such grandiose notions like 'our rightful place in the region/world' are not only inexact, they are actually dangerous on account of the xenophobia they breed. There is no such thing as a 'rightful' place. What 'right' are we referring to? Is it 'divine' right? Is it the 'right' guaranteed by military or economic power or by both? The 'jingoists' will no doubt refer to our large landmass, long history, huge population and our sub-continental configuration and the geographical location which we occupy on the East-West trade routes of the world to justify their claim for a 'rightful' place. We shall only say that such claims on the basis of history or geography are not valid. What are valid are concrete achievements like vast increase in GDP and in personal income, economic prosperity, military strength, political prestige and above all a happy and contented people who are united, regardless of the religion, caste or state they belong to or the language they speak. India is working towards this goal, just as China is working in its own way. Are we going to risk all that we have achieved in a mad race towards an illusory 'right'? Let us not be insane in our hurry to write our names on the pages of

History. Let us progress in an all-round manner, systematically and sincerely. All good things will come to us on their own!

Regarding border dispute, the apparatus to solve it was put in position years ago. We have made some progress in the dialogue with China. It may take many more rounds of talks to achieve results. But neither China nor India need be in undue haste to solve the dispute since by the 1993 Agreement on Border Peace and Tranquillity, we have defused the disputed areas issues to prevent any danger of explosion. The recent visit to India of Chinese Premier Wen Jiabao saw the formalisation of the 'Guiding Principles' to settle border dispute. The agreement signed on 12th April, 2005, states that the two countries were seeking a 'political solution' of the boundary question in the context of their overall long-term interests. The use of force or threatening the use of force was abjured. The spirit of mutual respect and mutual understanding must inform future negotiations, so that mutually acceptable adjustments to their respective positions on the boundary question could be made and a package solution arrived at. The settlement should be final, cover all sectors of boundary and safeguard due interests of their settled populations in the border areas. Significant progress indeed!

On balance, we feel that China, Russia and India could forge an alliance with security clauses to give us, collectively, a degree of immunity from the actions of the hegemon. Perhaps, this is what Chinese Premier Wen Jiabao had in mind when he told a group of journalists in New Delhi during his India visit that 'trilateral cooperation between India, China and Russia will help democratise international relations and safeguard world peace, security and stability'. The Agreement will also make Asia an excellent example of what nations can achieve, if they set their minds to it.

We shall leave our relations with the USA, Russia and China at this stage and see what foreign policy changes are required, in respect to the other countries of the world.

Our policies with Europe are sound. Perhaps we should be more wary of the UK as long as the present New Labour regime is in office. Their mindless toeing of the American policies towards Iraq and terrorism has been most unedifying from a country of such stature as it once had. Be that as it may, in Europe, we have many friends like France, Germany, Italy, the Low countries, Scandinavia, Eastern Europe and the countries on the shores of the Mediterranean. With them we should foster friendly relations and assist them in whatever manner they may want, e.g, the heavy demands for IT professionals. We should, however, take energetic steps to curb illegal migration from India to these countries as firm international friendships cannot be built if we allow our citizens to violate the laws of other countries. Among all the countries mentioned, France with its independent foreign policy, balanced armed forces, high levels of economic, scientific and technological achievements and above all, the freedom its citizens enjoy, comes closest to our idea of how we too may shape ourselves—only better!

The Central Asian Republics have been receiving less than adequate attention from South Block. Their gas and oil reserves are enormous and could form the basis of a meaningful two way commercial linkage. We should promote Indian investment in these countries in machine tools, farm machinery, consumer durables and so on and purchase from them gas and oil, having these transported by pipelines either via Pakistan or via Iran and under the Arabian Sea. We need to ensure that Russian sensitivities are kept in mind when we deal with the CARs.

With Afghanistan, we enjoy a historic friendship. Regardless of who ruled that country, India had always worked in Afghanistan's interests. Specially when the Taliban ruled, Indian support to the Northern Alliance was crucial in helping them to survive, move and fight. Eventually, it was the troops of the Northern Alliance which provided the *coup de grace* to the Taliban regime in Kabul. To military and political support, we must now add our wholehearted participation in the reconstruction of that war-ravaged country. Grants in aid, easy loans and lines of credit for Indian manufactured goods, direct Indian investments in their economy, promotion of joint ventures, undertaking infrastructure development projects and setting up factories, power plants, hospitals and so on, on a turn-key basis; all these should be examined. We should never lose sight of the fact that Kashmir has a land border with Afghanistan and that they are really our neighbours, even though Afghanistan is today a client state of the USA. Our present representatives in Afghanistan are doing good work and need to be encouraged and recognised.

Iran is another country which has had a stormy 50 years and seems set to receive more than its share of problems from the USA. The USA appears to have picked on Iran for her next target in its 'War on Terrorism'. Apparently the planners in the USA have decided that by making Pakistan a 'front line state' and a major non-NATO ally, virtually destroying Afghanistan and reconstructing it to their liking and doing likewise for Iraq (except that reconstruction seems a distant dream), they have virtually 'destroyed' terrorist hot beds in the West Asian region with one notable exception – Iran. So it seems that the tragedy of the US invasion of Iran is waiting to happen. India and the rest of the world should prevent such a plan from materialising. The hegemon must be stopped in its tracks by principled opposition in the Security Council and elsewhere. India should not get overly pleased with the USA calling us their 'ally' and speaking of 'Next Step in Strategic Progress' and military to military cooperation including low level, rather purposeless exercises and selling to us a few military equipments we wanted. All this is the sop that is being given to us to buy our silence while they carry out their invasion of Iran. History teaches us that Hitler could have been managed by the rest of Europe if the move to occupy Sudetenland had been resolutely opposed by them. They did not and we had the Polish invasion and World War II. Will we have to relearn History all over again? Once again, many will cavil at our portrayal of the USA as a rampaging hegemon. However, no other conclusion can be reached if one examines its track record in international relations. All of Latin America, the Balkans, most countries of East and South-East Asia, the Middle-East and North Africa, all have felt, at some time, the Machiavellian manoeuvres of the Central Intelligence Agency to destabilise a regime or provoke a rebellion against it or create conditions for the invasion of a small, weak country by the USA. Such an attack was launched against Nicaragua which, unable to defend itself, took the matter to the World Court. In 1986, the Court held the USA guilty of committing armed aggression against Nicaragua, ordered cessation of attacks and payment of reparations to the victim. The USA did not comply but escalated its attacks instead! Appeals by that unfortunate country to the UN Security Council and the General Assembly were fruitless. Does one need any clearer proof of the contempt for international law and propensity to use military force against any country baulking it, on the part of the superpower? It is quite clear that unless the world community unites to oppose its plans, the USA will find some excuse to attack Iran too and perhaps 'other states of concern' as its policy makers so euphemistically put it.

Our policy towards the countries of West Asia has been pragmatic and paid us fair dividends in terms of friendship with the Arabs as well as Israel. With the election of Mr. Mahmoud Abbas as Palestine Authority President and some hopeful signals emanating from Sharm-el-Shaik where Egyptian President Hosni Mobarak hosted the Israeli Prime Minister Sharon and Palestine leader Abbas to resume peace talks under the internationally agreed 'Road Map for Peace'. The USA has a vested interest in a West Asia peace as, indeed, we and the rest of the world have. A cessation of the endless cycle of terrorist attacks followed by Israeli retaliation, followed by fresh terrorist attacks and so on 'ad nauseam' must be arrested. Our effort must be to work for a durable peace in the region. We should also step up trade and economic cooperation with the countries of the region. However, till such time as the general violence level in the region dies down – which we assess will only be after the US and its allies remove their military presence from Iraq and some form of truce is agreed upon between Israel on the one hand and Palestine Authority on the other – we should discourage our citizens seeking work in that region.

Our relations with countries of Africa have been marked by enlightened self-interest on our part. We supported freedom movements in various countries, the anti-apartheid struggle in South Africa and participated with great distinction in UN peace keeping operations in various countries such as the Congo, Sierra Leone, Somalia, Ethiopia and Eritrea. We have also ongoing security training programmes in Botswana, Mauritius and earlier on, in Nigeria. We need to foster closer economic links with these countries and work for the success of the Indian Ocean Rim Association's objectives. Our relations with South Africa have benefited by our purchase of military equipment from that country. We should, in time, work towards joint manufacture of such defence equipment for mutual benefit. This nascent relationship cannot but be adversely affected by the mid-May media revelations, alleging use of middlemen and illegal payments in a projected purchase by India of some weapons from South Africa.

Latin America has not received much attention from our Foreign Office. With Brazil aspiring to become a permanent member of the Security Council and the impressive economic growth of some of the Latin American countries, our presence and interest in the region must be stepped up. Our special relations with the Caribbean states of Guyana and Trinidad-Tobago with their cultural linkages to India, must be strengthened. Perhaps, as our own economy burgeons and we search the world for new markets, Latin America may be an important destination for us to visit. Peru can become an alternative or supplementary source for crude oil.

The current 'Look East' policy, whose enunciation was almost synchronous with our policy of economic liberalisation, was long overdue. Now that it is in full operation, beneficial results have already started accruing to us. Among these must be counted our new relationship with the ASEAN Regional Forum, the increased investment in India by some of Asian 'Tigers', notably Singapore, growth of joint ventures with Malaysia, Singapore, Thailand and Indonesia and the increased interest being displayed by Japan towards India as an investment destination. Even with South Korea, our economic relations have taken an upswing with their major industrial companies like Hyundai, Daewoo and Samsung collaborating with Indian companies to manufacture their products in India. Our effort must be directed towards further growth of our economic relations with these countries, the development of cooperation in ensuring the safety of maritime trade, cooperation in anti-piracy measures and in 'Search and Rescue' missions over the oceans. We also need to evolve a strategic relationship with these countries so that our views on world affairs may achieve greater congruence and thus prove more decisive.

We have mentioned China earlier in the context of a security arrangement. An economically resurgent China is already flooding the world markets with cheap, manufactured goods ranging from toys to aircraft. Our economic and trade relations with China are, however, miniscule. Stepping up our bilateral trade and setting up joint ventures with China would be a very beneficial measure towards bringing the two countries closer. The great interest shown by Chinese leaders in India's Information Technology industry must be capitalised on and our companies helped to set up operations in China. Chinese Premier Wen Jiabao made his views on Sino-Indian technological cooperation quite clear in his statements in Bangalore on 10th April, 2005. He told the audience at Tata Consultancy Services (TCS), "I strongly believe if India and China join hands, we will certainly be able to set a new trail in the IT business world, which will signify the coming of the Asian century of the IT industry". And again, noting India's great prowess in software and China's progress in hardware, he said, "Cooperation is just like two pagodas—one hardware and one software — and combined, we can take the leadership position in the world." All that we wish to add is "Amen."

Finally, we come to Australia, New Zealand and Oceania. Staunch allies of the USA, these countries maintain low key but cordial relations with us. There is a sizeable population of Indian expatriates in Australia, Fiji and so on and they have played an useful role in ensuring cordial relations with us. There is a great deal of interest in Australia about India. We need to capitalise on this and give a major boost to our bilateral trade with these countries. As of now, cricket and coking coal seem to be the points of convergence between us and Australia and New Zealand! This can surely be diversified and enriched in content.

Despite some criticism, the foreign policy of India has been pragmatic and designed to create a favourable international environment in which we may pursue our national goals of rapid economic development, eradication of poverty and promotion of prosperity and happiness among our people. Such an environment cannot be created unless we are strong both economically and militarily and develop the ability to manage our relations with our neighbours in a harmonious manner. It is no secret that our relations with Pakistan have been terrible since the birth of that country though it seems there may be some improvement in the coming days. Likewise, with Bangladesh too, we have had a patchy relationship which can be corrected only if there is a will to do so on both sides of the border. SAARC, launched with such fanfare some years ago, appears to have become moribund and will need an infusion of faith and hard work by its members to save it from perishing. However, the entire region will benefit if the countries decide to engage one another more vigorously in trade, commerce and other economic activity, laying aside long standing problems for the present to be taken up later. There appears to be no alternative to letting sound economic and foreign policies converge to create an environment of peace and security in the region and, indeed, in the world.

9

Pakistan's Military
A Psychological Profile

Whether a country is engaged in war with another country or when both countries are holding peace talks, it is imperative that one should be aware of what makes the other side 'tick'; what is the mainspring of their national power, motivation, their hopes and their despair. We have fought three wars with Pakistan – four, if you include the Kargil fighting and five, if you also count the proxy war launched by them in J&K, 14 years ago. Now, there is talk of peace. Officially, there is a ceasefire all along our common frontiers. There have been discussions and meetings at various levels, from Pakistan's President and Indian Prime Minister, to between military officers of both sides. Our cricket team toured Pakistan last year and their team toured our country this year. The rattling of sabres is no longer heard. The rhetoric has become subdued. Indians and Pakistanis, from the high and mighty to the common man or woman, are being very 'nice' to each other, friendly and as free with their compliments to the other side as they were with their imprecations a couple of years ago.

But we err. On our side of the fence, our redoubtable Don Quixotes, unable to find suitable windmills at which to 'tilt', found a substitute target in the Mohali cricket pitch! What fantastic flexibility, what unparalleled patriotism, how great a contribution they made to our national honour and prestige! We believed till the 'Mohali Incident,' that the Jurassic Age ended a long time ago. However, the excavation of the Mohali cricket pitch at the start of the recently concluded Pakistan cricket tour of India, strongly suggested that this was the handiwork of creatures with poorly developed brains, large muscles, high blood pressure, hyper-active adrenals and total deficiency of logic processes; not human certainly, possibly Saurians. But then, maybe, we are being unfair to our remote predecessors on this planet! What a shame! What an utterly uncivilized action! But these evolutionary throwbacks do occur from time to time and we have to take them in our stride. In any case, cricket lovers in India turned up in their hundreds of thousands to watch various India-Pakistan matches including the Delhi match which Pakistan's President Musharraf watched alongside Prime Minister Manmohan Singh. India lost; but Cricket won over ultra-nationalism.

Returning to the modern era, most political scientists from all over the world, attach very great importance to the role of the Pakistan Army in every facet of their national life. In fact, the centrality of the Pakistan Army to that country dates back to 14th August, 1947, when Pakistan was born and continues till date. During this period of 58 years, Pakistan has been ruled by the Army in four spells totaling up to 32 years – roughly 55 per cent of the time since its birth. These four spells were:

- Field Marshal Ayub Khan, from 27th October, 1958, to 25th March, 1969.

- **General** Yahya Khan, from 25th March, 1969, to 16th December, 1971.
- General Zia ul Haq, from 5th July, 1977, to 17th August, 1988.
- General Pervez Musharraf, from 12th October, 1999, to 21st October, 2002. However, even after the latter date, the General continues to be effectively the chief arbiter of Pakistan as he is both the Chief of the Pakistan Army and the President of the country.

We need to take note of the fact that the Pakistan Army has been a vital pillar of Pakistan's polity, the others being the feudal gentry, the clergy and the bureaucracy. After repeated spells of Army rule and the generally poor contribution made by the other three pillars of Pakistani society, the country has come to look upon its Army as their saviours. This, they have certainly been, barring the tragic run of events from 25th March, 1971, till over a year later in July 1972, when the Shimla Agreement was signed, leading to the repatriation of a large number of Pakistani prisoners-of-war in Indian custody since 1971. Despite that period when the people of Pakistan held their army rulers responsible for the breaking away of the Eastern wing of the country to become a free country, Bangladesh, the Pakistan Army still retained its primacy in the hierarchy of power in the country. This speaks eloquently of the very high esteem which the Army is held in by the people of Pakistan – regarded in fact, as the saviour of the young state—to a greater extent than other peoples regard their armies. There are historical reasons for this phenomenon which left an indelible imprint on the psyche of Pakistan's military in general and the Army in particular.

Let us first deal with the soldiers. Before 1947, the recruitment of soldiers for the 'old' Indian Army was on the basis of the dogma of 'martial races' enunciated by the British. From well before the historic watershed year of 1857, the Army in India recruited soldiers on the basis of availability for the Bengal, Madras and Bombay 'Armies', and as the domain administered by the British expanded, the availability of recruitable population too expanded. For an army of finite size, therefore, more selective recruitment became feasible. This led the recruiters (generally the officers of the battalion) to prefer 'larger men to those who were smaller, men accustomed to extremes of temperature and easy to train'. Philip Mason, in his classic, *A Matter of Honour,* states, "Height, weight, conformation and disposition – all these would be taken into account. Just as he might prefer Arab horses or Kathiawari or Australian, he would prefer men of one region, speech and religion". Post-1857, there was also a preference for the 'good', rather than the 'bad' or 'unreliable' Indian.

In 1880, Lord Roberts was appointed Commander-in-Chief of the Madras Army. He opined that "Madrassies as a rule are more intelligent and better educated than the fighting races of Northern India" and concluded that they would make better sappers or Pioneers than Infantry. He gave effect to this when he was C-in-C, Madras Army, and continued with this dispensation when he became C-in-C of the Bengal Army in 1885, with supervisory powers over both the Madras and Bombay Armies. By the time he left India in 1893, the system of region or class based recruitment, which he so strongly believed in, had become an established practice. At the turn of the 19th century, recruitment of soldiers was basically from Gurkhas, Sikhs, Dogras, Rajputs, Jats and select 'Mahommadens' such as the Punjabi Muslim, the Baluch and some Pathans. The recruitment of 'Madrassies' other than the Coorgs, Marathas, Bengalis, Muslims from east of the River

Yamuna, other Indian states of today and Sindhis had virtually died down to a trickle. The former group were the 'martial classes' and the latter 'the non-martial classes'. Lord Roberts also wrote as his 'parting shot', that Indian troops, though excellent, needed to be led and that Indian officers were not good enough to do so independently – 'they needed a British officer to support them in time of difficulty'.

We do not wish to make any comment on the validity or otherwise of the views of Lord Roberts except to state that the soldiery of both India and Pakistan have inherited their self-belief and conviction of their military superiority from Lord Roberts. In Pakistan, the recruitment pattern has not changed much, while in India, it is more in accord with the demography of the country. Thus, the Pakistani soldier, since the birth of that country, has been brought up in the belief that 'one Pakistani equalled ten or twenty Hindu Indian soldiers' as stated by Stephen Philip Cohen in his recent book *The Idea of Pakistan*. Needless to say that the events of 1971 overthrew both the martial race theory and the 'human resource equation'.

The 'martial classes' concept certainly continued to be followed in Pakistan. Whereas the Punjabis, Baluchis and Pathans continued to be highly sought after in recruitment rallies and so on, Sindhis, Bengalis and candidates from Pakistan Occupied Kashmir were less favoured. Whereas the Air Force and the Navy accepted the Bengalis and Sindhis freely, the Army was tardy in accepting them in the Infantry. The Occupied Kashmir recruits were assigned to one 'Azad Kashmir' Regiment and the militia, 'Northern Light Infantry'. The enrolment of officers was generally on an All-Pakistan basis but with the Punjabi officer dominating. Thus, we have a Pakistani soldiery which has developed the following characteristics:

- Very high self-belief; this has been toned down by the force of events from their self-deluding belief in their over-riding superiority over India's Army to a more pragmatic assessment of their opponents.
- Great pride in their physical fitness, skill at arms, tactical prowess and determination in battle.
- Dash and daring under favourable circumstances.
- Tendency to seek their officers' guidance and directions in all but simple situations.
- Lack of initiative under difficult circumstances when officer/leadership is either not present or is ineffective.
- A sense of being 'second class' entries into the Army among persons enrolled from Occupied Kashmir, including the 'Northern Areas'. This is clearly shown by the manner in which many battalions of the Northern Light Infantry reacted to the Pakistan GHQ's order that the fiction of there being no troops' involvement in the Kargil aggression in 1999, be maintained by refusing to accept bodies of slain NLI soldiers, sought to be handed over by India. Not only was this the worst kind of manmanagement, it was a reprehensible and inhuman act.
- A sense of grievance against their officers among many troops deployed along the Line of Control suggests that troops do not think highly of officers not visiting them oftener and sharing their privations while on active service.
- A sense of disappointment with their logistic support was also noticed among forward troops on a number of occasions when they seemed to have no tea or sugar or some such item of troops' rations. On many occasions, in quiet sectors,

Indian troops had freely shared such items of their own rations with Pakistani soldiers on being requested by them.

These are some of the observed traits of the soldiers of Pakistan Army today. They are, overall, average soldiers who are physically tough, self confident and generally display dash and daring when the circumstances are in their favour. They show lack of initiative and steadiness under difficult circumstances unless they are resolutely led by good officers. There is a perceptible gap between officers and troops, and the logistic support system in forward areas is not always satisfactory. There is a sense of 'neglect' among some troops as they are considered 'second class' citizens.

Let us now take a look at the officer class of the Pakistan Army.

- The intake into the Pakistan Military Academy which is the basic officer training establishment of the Army, is about 350 to 400 every year. The bulk of the intake – i.e over 65 per cent, is from Punjab; the North West Frontier Province contributes about 15 per cent, Sindh 10 per cent, Baluchistan 5 per cent and Occupied Kashmir about 2 per cent. There are a number of Urdu speaking officers whose ancestors migrated from India around 1947, like the President, General Musharraf. All others speak the language of their states and English. A good number of Pakistani officers have studied Arabic, Persian, Russian, Chinese and Afghani languages.
- Of the 300 or so who graduate from PMA each year, about half (150) attain the rank of Colonel and, of these, some 90 will go on to one and two star ranks. Only about 20 officers will attain 3-star rank. The officers who leave the service at any

stage for reasons other than misconduct or grave offences, are generally absorbed in the civilian services or para military forces. In overall terms, though the career progression in the Army is 'pyramidal', the level of satisfaction is maintained at a reasonable mark by lateral absorption of early retirees. There is, therefore, no dearth of candidates for selection to the PMA with approximately 15,000 youngmen of age 17 to 22 years, applying every year for about 300 cadets to be selected – a 'culling' rate of about one in 500. Over the years, the number of candidates from the wealthy or feudal classes has dwindled while that of servicemen's sons, specially Junior Commissioned Officers' sons, has significantly increased. In an Army with the robust traditions of the Pakistan Army, the intake, whatever be his social background, is soon transformed into an average Pakistani officer.

- The average Pakistani officer is little different from the average Indian Army officer – at least, during and immediately after pre-commission training. He comes from a middle class family, looks upon the Army as a career which will give him prestige, an adventurous life and the wherewithal to support his parents who are ageing and put his younger siblings through college and so on. He also has the urge to excel in sports, military training and studies and is a keen competitor. He is one Muslim among a large number of them and he follows the tenets of his Faith in the manner that most youths do – quietly and without any public parading of his commitment to it; in fact, as a part of his personal duty to his Creator. He thinks often about his country's circumstances and what ails its polity and economy. He probably has his heroes, though most of them at the PMA are more likely to have the great fast bowler Shoaib Akhtar as their hero rather than Kamal Ataturk who was President Musharraf's role model. His political views are still not fully formed though he firmly believes that India is Enemy No. 1 and would like to undo Pakistan, wages non-stop 'pogroms' against Muslims in India and wishes to become the regional hegemon and a great power. He hopes that by the time he attends the Staff College at Quetta and the National Defence College at Islamabad, he would know what to do about India. For the present, he works and plays hard and hopes he will be commissioned into the Regiment of his choice. Stephen Philip Cohen in his book '*The Idea of Pakistan*' avers, "In India it is widely and incorrectly believed that from about this date (1971) onward, all cadets at the Pakistan Military Academy were required to take an oath swearing revenge against India for the loss of East Pakistan". We are glad to read his categoric and authoritative words, for it would have been a shame for young minds to be deliberately poisoned with thoughts like revenge, etc.

- Post-commissioning, the Pakistan Army officer will do a number of tenures in forward areas opposite India, in the J&K sector or the Siachen Glacier sector. These postings with his battalion and the experiences he undergoes, shape his military attitudes and thought processes. Repeated exposure to the ISI run trans-border terrorist infiltration makes him regard 'terrorism' as a legitimate weapon for use against the Indians. It also makes him develop some idea of the power wielded by the ISI. Cross-border exchanges of fire including that of artillery and mortars, some exchanges lasting a few days, harden him and make him a seasoned soldier. It is here that he may gain or lose the respect and affection of his men, depending on how closely he identifies himself with the soldier or how self-absorbed he is. We believe the average Indian officer fares better than his Pakistani counterpart in this regard (as, indeed, the Pakistani officer might be thinking about the Indian). He attends the usual training courses, goes abroad too on either UN missions or training courses or deputation to an Arab country or some other official assignment and develops good communication skills and knowledge about the countries visited by him. In his own country, he sees that the Army wields tremendous power while politicians seem to him to be an 'endangered species', unable to save themselves, let alone serve Pakistan! He develops an aversion to them. He has a little more 'time' for bureaucrats but not a great deal of respect as they serve the 'master-of-the day'. These attitudes and his personal observations of the events the country is going through, make him politically aware and 'concerned'. The more ambitious or more politically minded among them would be conscious of their all-round superiority over the 'civilians' by virtue of their professionalism, training, their versatility in handling any job, including civilian jobs and doing it better than the civilian and by his better understanding of the people's problems and needs at the grassroots level, because his own troops are from that slice of society. He knows too that he is patriotic, honest and competent and that the politician is the opposite of all that he is. Given the right circumstances such as the situation that developed on 12th October, 1999, when General Pervez Musharraf ousted the then Prime

> Minister Nawaz Sharif, the Pakistani Army Officer is likely to lead a *coup d'etat*. The fact that all Army led coups, till date, barring the September 1995 attempt by Major General Zahir-ul-Islam Abbasi, were entirely successful, suggests that the coups were acceptable to the people at large and within the three services as well. This will always be contested by the ousted politicians but, *they* did not provide the leadership Pakistan needed; so, reluctantly the Army stepped in and ruled for a long time thereafter!

A word about the influence of religion on the Army and what the present trends in this regard indicate for the future of the Pakistan Army: Islam has always been a motivating force for the Pakistan Army. It seems to be '*de rigueur*' in an Islamic state. However, contrary to many assessments on the subject made by various eminent soldiers, diplomats and writers from time to time, we believe that Islam has not completely supplanted the professional ethos of the Army. Except during General Zia ul Haq's regime when there were many reports about the 'Tablighi Jamaat', operating freely within the Army and preaching to its personnel and the brief introduction of Islamic criteria for recruitment or promotion by General Aslam Beg (General Zia's successor), there was no institutionalised attempt to promote greater religious fervour within the Army than what was achieved by the regimental Maulvi and the individual soldier's own upbringing. Even Aslam Beg's attempt to Islamise further, was annulled by his successor General Asif Nawaz Janjua. From this, it would be clear that religious influence within the Army has been kept at a moderate level. In any case, the more radical Islamic groups such as the Wahabis of Saudi Arabia and Jamaat-e-Islami, a political party, were not allowed to carry out their work within the ranks of the

Army. We believe this situation obtains till today and should continue under the policies of the present Pakistani regime.

This does not, however, mean that some individuals have not become attracted to radical versions of Islam. Many soldiers and officers of the Pakistan Army have served in Saudi Arabia and would presumably have come into contact with 'Wahabism' – the same 'ism' that 'rabidized' the Taliban and the Al Qaeda. We do not know whether these personnel have turned radical in their beliefs; however, some would have, while others may have been only partly affected. All of them however, who served for two to three years in Saudi Arabia would be 'comfortable' with the radical Islamists they might meet in Pakistan though they may not follow their precepts. We have to also remember that the Islamic Revolution in Iran (1979), the fighting by the various Afghan groups including the deeply fundamentalist Jamaat-e-Islami and the strong support given by Pakistan to the Taliban regime (1990-2003), all influenced the rank and file of the Pakistan Army to some extent. Those who were actually involved as volunteers in the fighting and those who, as functionaries of the ISI were responsible for dealing directly with the various Mujahideen groups, would have come under radical Islam's influence. Some of them are in senior ranks in the Pakistan Army today. A further complicating factor that has now assumed more importance than ever before, is the increasing propensity of the Pakistan regime to use Islamic radical organisations for their own purposes, basically to 'spike the guns' of the Pakistan Peoples' Party and the Muslim League. This is not good augury as two provinces have become virtually 'talibanised' after the electoral triumphs of the Islamic political parties (Baluchistan and NWFP). If this trend continues and radical Islam gains further adherents, the

'Doomsday' warning which was put out in the *New Indian Express* of 14th February, 2005, may well become a reality. The report, warns of a "Yugoslavia-like fate" for Pakistan by 2015. Based on an assessment, jointly prepared by the United States National Intelligence Council (NIC) and the CIA, the operative part of the assessment reads, "by the year 2015, Pakistan would be a failed state, ripe with civil war, bloodshed, inter-provincial rivalries and a struggle for control of its nuclear weapons and complete talibanisation". This is indeed a grim prospect.

So far, whenever Pakistan seemed to be headed for disaster, the Army would step in and set matters right for the time being. Today, Pakistan is a 'front line state' in the US led war against terrorism. It is also a major non-NATO ally of the USA. Within Pakistan, two provinces have shown their preference for an Islamic ruling order. Sind, as always, seems to be in a ferment, while Occupied Kashmir has not experienced normalcy for over 50 years, even though there is talk of more porous borders with India's J&K State. The heartland of Pakistan, Punjab, is riven by sectarian clashes and there is not a week when terrorist outrages do not occur. Politicians who matter, stand exiled or jailed. Within a period of five years since he took over the country, President Musharraf has cleared the decks for his own unfettered rule with the help of loyal, handpicked Army officers, bureaucrats of proven ability and unstinted support from the USA. What could pose his rule the greatest danger are radical Islamic parties/groups or the return of some of the political 'heavyweights'. Only time will tell whether the Pakistan Army, through the medium of General Musharraf, will weather the storms that are looming ahead or, as given in the US NIC-CIA joint assessment, will Pakistan 'fail' as a state and lapse into utter chaos. Our reading of the psyche of the Pakistan Army suggests to us that Pakistan will survive, thanks to the Pakistan Army.

10

India's Soldier

We have touched on a great number of subjects and talked of all kinds of people in this book – politicians, diplomats, bureaucrats, terrorists, Pakistan's Army et al. We shall now turn our attention to the most important person who features in this book – India's Soldier.

'Jawan', as he is affectionately called, India's soldier is worth far more than a chapter in this or any other book. He is a book by himself. He represents all of India and India is too vast in every physical and non-physical dimension to be captured in even a whole library full of books. Our Jawan is a microcosmic model of India and mere books cannot do justice to him. His life will merit a lifetime of study.

But the focus on the Jawan here is not for the purpose of singing his praises. It is for the purpose of familiarising ourselves with his entire service life, from his recruitment to his retirement and to his final departure from the world. The objective in doing so is to see that as a Nation, we express our gratitude to him in a concrete, meaningful manner, make his life as free from worries as possible and try to add to his morale and strength by backing him wholeheartedly with all the available resources, at all times. He deserves all this and more, for he is India's frontline soldier, India's flag-bearer and defender.

Recruitment of soldiers is undertaken at regular intervals under the aegis of the Adjutant General through the network of Zonal and Branch Recruiting Offices. This process, where most would-be-soldiers come into contact for the first time with the Army, used to be a nightmarish experience for the organisers and candidates alike. It also used to be a very profitable period for touts and racketeers of various sorts who exploited the huge gap between the number of candidates and vacancies available. A great deal has been done to keep the touts away from recruitment rallies. However, the lure of easy money still persuades some enterprising fellows to ply their sordid trade as before, but with far greater circumspection and, regrettably, some 'inside' assistance. Unless the loopholes that still exist are plugged and all personnel in the recruiting organisation are selected with great care, these touts will continue to plague the rally grounds, looking for a few gullible candidates or their kinfolk, to dupe and relieve them of their money.

The rally grounds themselves are often a sad spectacle. Usually, candidates are asked to report at the rally ground by 6 AM or so. Most candidates and their guardians, therefore, arrive the previous night and rough it out at the railway station, bus stand or some such place where they may spend the night and reach the rally ground on time. Since even small districts have large recruitable male populations and the Army is a very attractive profession, the crowds that arrive for recruiting rallies are enormous. This leads to many undesirable consequences. There is a lot of pushing and shoving to get up ahead of the others; at times a stampede occurs. A few years ago, a large number of candidates and their guardians sat on a large cemented surface, little realising that it was a poorly constructed sewage tank cover. The result was that the cover collapsed and many were hurt. Perhaps, there is no need to construct elaborate facilities for such rallies. But some essential arrangements must be made by the local administration in consultation with the Army Recruiting Organisation. These include selection of a suitable rally ground, sanitation facilities for candidates and their guardians, provision of clean drinking water and suitably positioned public address system for announcements to guide candidates from place to place.

Some points relating to the process that a candidate undergoes for recruitment, are given here for guidance of both the recruiting organisation and the candidates:

- Every effort should be made to so manage the checking of documents and taking of physical measurements of candidates that the physical tests that follow are conducted at a convenient time of the day and certainly not at noon on a hot summer day.
- The candidates who are eliminated after the physical tests should be dispersed in an orderly manner and not allowed to 'mill' around the venue.
- The medical tests follow the established procedure. However, it is surprising how many candidates are required to get their ears cleaned at a named private facility in town for a fat fee! Can the Army not position their own ENT personnel for rallies as a matter of routine?
- The medical examinations conclude on the second day and successful candidates are told to return on a specified date, a week or so hence, to appear

for their written examination. The question papers are printed in Roman Hindustani. That would be alright if the candidate is familiar with the Hindustani part of it. However, many candidates are unable to follow the Hindi used in the question paper. In large parts of Southern India, Hindi is scarcely taught and a boy of 16 or 17 years of age may have hardly any useful Hindi vocabulary and certainly no grammar! In fairness to all candidates, the written test should be such that a candidate understands the questions and is at liberty to answer in his mother tongue if he has no Hindi or English competence. Perhaps, some multi-lingual personnel who can verbally explain the questions for the benefit of all, should be detailed to assist in the conduct of written examination.

- Candidates have to disperse after the written examination and again reassemble after a few days to find out whether they figure in the merit list or not. An otherwise very fit candidate who has not done well in the written examination could be asked to reappear only for that examination after, say, 15-20 days and enroll with the next batch.
- Successful candidates go home and arrive on the appointed day at the Branch Recruiting Office, to join a squad or draft. They are then given a warrant for railway journey to reach their regimental training centre.
- On arrival at the destination, the recruit either makes his own way to the training centre or avails of military vehicles attending trains at the railway station. Finally, he enters the place that will transform him from a recruit into a trained soldier, to take his place in the ranks of India's Army. Let us see what happens to him at the Training Centre.

The Regimental Centres are responsible for the 'basic' and 'advanced' training of recruits in a period of approximately 45-53 weeks. After successfully completing his training, the recruit takes the oath of loyalty and obedience at an Attestation Parade which makes him a young soldier. He is then assigned to a unit of his Regiment – an armoured regiment, infantry battalion, field regiment (Artillery) and so on, to embark on his chosen career as a soldier. But all that lies in the future. Let us first see what happens to our recruit who arrives by a private bus at the gates of his Regimental Centre.

He has 'recruit' written all over him, as it were. He is far away from his village, among strangers, except for 14 others who had travelled with him from the Recruiting Centre to the Regimental Centre. He finds the spick and span appearance of the gate and the guard room intimidating. He looks lost. Not for long though, as an NCO is deputed to take him to the Recruits' Reception and Despatch Centre (RRDC). This journey from the gate to RRDC is perhaps of half a kilometer and is completed at the 'double' with his baggage being carried by him. Before even giving him a chance to catch his breath, he is told to leave his baggage on the ground outside RRDC and is doubled off to get his hair-cut. There is a story one hears in most training centres that the barbers employed there are from the Australian outback and experts at shearing sheep. They make short work of our new arrival who is then taken to the RRDC. Here, his documents are checked and he is told what he may do (obey orders) and what he may not do (anything else). He is then familiarised with the layout of the Centre by an NCO who shows the group the firing ranges, different training regiments, institutes, married quarters, barracks for recruits and so on. If he gets any time off at all, it is for a 15 minutes break just before roll-call parade at 1900 hrs. During these 15 minutes, he puts away the kit he has been issued during the running tour of the Centre and if possible, washes the grime off himself. Roll calls are used for a variety of purposes and promulgation of orders is one of them. The new recruit is bewildered by the entire proceedings he has been 'caught up' in but he says to himself that it will become alright, by and by. He, like most young people from villages, is an optimist and this helps him to take everything in his stride. He sleeps in a barrack in the RRDC complex along with his fellow recruits after dinner– a substantial meal – but not before he has managed to bathe. Even before he can say his prayers or think of writing a letter to his parents, he is fast asleep.

Life begins well before dawn at the Training Centres. By the time the bugles sound the 'reveille', our recruit has done a lot of work. Having washed and dressed, he has appeared before three or four 'seniors' for being inspected. The fact is that he has to fetch them their tea. He takes it in good spirit. Then, along with his fellow recruits, he sweeps and swabs the barracks and ensures that there are no fallen leaves or anything of that nature in the area around the barrack. Very early in his career he learns that 'Cleanliness is next to Godliness' and that he must take personal pride in sprucing up — himself and his barracks.

During the day, the recruit is allotted a personal number, is photographed and answers questions that he is asked by a JCO or clerk to get his 'long roll' completed. He also visits the Regimental shops and buys some essential articles such as boot polish, blanco, brushes, brasso, personal toilet requisites and so on. He also buys a large sized black steel trunk, the like of which everyone in India would have seen at the innumerable railway stations of our vast country, bearing a soldier's personal number and his name, indicating that the soldier himself is somewhere nearby.

In addition to all this, the recruit has to sign a number of papers in relation to his terms of service, nomination of next of kin and so on. He also does a lot of touring of the Centre, always at the double, and sees what activities go on in that rather busy place. All this takes about a week, at the end of which the recruit has been kitted up fully, has 'done' his basic documentation, has a fair idea of what is in store for him in the weeks ahead and, above all, has already developed some new friendships with his mates, friendships born out of experiences shared, hardships undergone and jokes exchanged. Such friendships are the early stirrings of the mutual bonding of soldiers which we call 'camaraderie'. Without 'camaraderie', an army cannot hope to become a winning team.

The next 19 weeks or so are devoted to 'basic' training. The recruit has left the RRDC and has been assigned to a regiment, let us say, 2 Training Regiment. Here, he and his squad mates are assigned to an NCO in charge and stay in his barrack. For all purposes, that NCO is '*in loco parentis*' to our 16 years old recruit and depending on how he handles his squad, the recruits will develop well or not so well. The routine in the Training Regiment is taxing. The pre-dawn rituals continue. There are hours of Physical Training (PT), Drill, Weapon Training (WT) and Hindi classes. For each of these, there are specialist instructors and the training areas are far apart in the campus. The recruit is constantly on the run from one event to another, now in PT kit, then ready for WT with his rifle. He snatches his standard breakfast of 'puries' and tea in the brief interval between PT and Drill and by the time he reaches the Hindi classroom, he is looking forward to lunch. Probably that is why he often dozes off during the class and earns for his lapse a round of the football field, at the double, naturally. The recruits have a great deal of work to do in the post-lunch period. There is the never-ending requirement of 'maintaining' the area with primitive tools (early Iron Age, we hear) and the need to clean, paint or polish something or the other. There are 'working' parties on which he is detailed, ranging from collection of dry rations to clearing out the dry storm water drains; from sprucing up the Regimental institutes to watering the extensive flower-beds. The recruit does it all and the Centre looks the better for his ministrations. Thus, this 16-year-old learns the dignity of hard work and the underlying truth that more 'hands' means 'lighter' work. He also learns to 'let off steam' in private by *sotto voce* comments to his mates. So the 'basic' training progresses for all of the mandated 20 weeks (including the week in RRDC) and our recruit, now a bit taller, a bit leaner, but more muscular and a lot more sure of himself, appears for various physical proficiency tests, drill tests, WT test and the inevitable Hindi test. Our recruit does well and qualifies in all the tests and is extremely happy when he is handed over his railway warrant and some advance of pay and is asked to proceed on 'Recruits Leave' for 28 days.

When he reaches his village after a three-day train journey involving two changes of trains, he cannot help walking taller and looking more mature and self-confident. The three weeks, which is all that he gets to spend at home, (the to and fro journey taking away six days) is also useful to the family. He helps his brothers to rethatch the barn and retile the roof of their house. He also helps his father to dig new watercourses in their field and create a new humus pit for farmyard waste and leaves. These three weeks pass off fast, days of happy toil with his kith and kin, long chats with his folks under the stars and telling everyone at home about his training and his immediate future. Now it's time for our recruit to take leave of his folks who fight away their tears when he catches the bus for the railway junction to board the train. Our recruit also wipes his eyes but tells his co-passengers that a particle of dust has fallen in his eye! They nod tolerantly and smile – after all, the boy is just 16 years of age or a bit older, they feel.

Our recruit on return is happy to meet his old mates but becomes sad when he finds that out of the original 15 of his squad, only six will be with him in 3 Training Regiment to which he has been assigned, the remaining eight staying on in 2 Training Regiment for the Advanced Training for the next 20 weeks or so. At the end of that period, as General Duties Soldiers, their training period of 44 weeks will end and they will be assigned to the units to which they will belong for the rest of their service lives.

Advanced training helps our recruit to graduate to a higher rung in the learning process. He works at his PT so that he can achieve excellent results in Battle Physical Efficiency Tests. He learns how to fire his rifle and light machine gun, how to throw a grenade, and the art of stalking and tactical use of ground. He learns about field defences, the routines in defence and attack operations and the art of patrolling. He also learns to do all this by day and night. He drills with his rifle to his Drill Instructor's (DI) satisfaction and that is saying a lot as the tribe of DIs are seldom satisfied. He learns also to camp out, put up tents and bivouacs, dig snake-pits and do speed marches from point-to-point, running the entire course of 21 kilometers. Overall, our recruit, now fully two centimeters taller than when he enlisted, looks very fit and trim and full of self-confidence, and is easily able to negotiate all the tests at the end of 44 weeks, all except Hindi where his instructor pushes him through with some grace marks.

There is a gap of almost two weeks after the end of the training as the batch which joined five days after them also joins them at the Attestation Parade. During this period our recruit is temporarily assigned to act as the Adjutant's Orderly, a position in which he acquits himself with rare distinction. He also parades with everyone for the Attestation Parade practices. Finally, almost a full year after he entered the portals of his Regimental Training Centre as a raw recruit, our young soldier leaves for the railway station, together with his friends to join his battalion located in Sikkim at an altitude of nearly 3500 metres above mean sea level. The journey across the country takes almost six days with three train changes and a long bus journey before the soldier reaches the Acclimatisation Camp, a few kilometres ahead of Gangtok. After seven days of acclimatisation in two stages, he reports his arrival in his battalion.

Our soldier, we shall call him Raj for ease of reference, is assigned to 'A' company, which has just then started their second individual training cycle of 12 weeks in their permanent location, on a massive, craggy feature which we shall call 'Fort'. Raj joins in all their activities with great enthusiasm. Rock climbing, firing uphill or down-hill, handling of mines and wire obstacles, field craft, map reading and a host of other skills are acquired by him. He is also given an extra dose of duties in the Guard-Room as normally happens with all 'juniors' and is considered to be excellent in demonstrating 'challenging' by the night sentry. Raj earnes his spurs in the Company when another soldier slips down and falls into a rocky chute and Raj, without any hesitation, volunteers to rescue him. And so it goes on in 'A' Company with Raj becoming clearly visible to everyone, as possible leadership material.

Raj is a natural marksman. It is, therefore, no surprise to anyone that he attends the Platoon Weapons NCOs Course at Mhow and comes back with an Instructor's rating. He also achieves excellence in PT and does the PT Course at the Army School of Physical Training, Pune. In the interim, his unit moves from Sikkim to Punjab and from there, twice again, once to Arunachal Pradesh and thence to J&K for counter-insurgency operations. Nearly 10 years have passed since Raj enlisted. He is a Naik now, a Section Second-in-Command in counter-insurgency operations, looked up to by all his comrades, seniors and juniors alike and widely regarded as a future Subedar Major of the Battalion. Fate, unfortunately, wills it otherwise.

Three months after his induction into the J&K Sector, Raj is part of a cordon and search operation in the area of Handwara. In the early hours of the morning, just when everyone in the cordon has got into his appointed place, there is a burst of hostile machine gun fire from a house on the outskirts of the village that has been cordoned. A burst of machine gun fire hits Raj in the right thigh, flinging him to the ground. Raj is caught standing on his feet in a hostile area and pays the price for it. He has lost pints of blood and eventually his entire right leg above the knee. All because he stands up to move to the platoon HQ to speak to his Section Commander who had been called there already. He is evacuated by helicopter to the Military Hospital at Srinagar and after being stabilised, by air to Army Hospital (Research and Referral) in the capital for further treatment. He has to be fitted with a prosthetic limb at the Army's Artificial Limb Centre, Pune, and almost two years after his injury, he is delighted to be able to meet the train of his Battalion's Main Body at Pune to which the Battalion has been deinducted from J&K. He is still on his feet and able to walk with his old 'A' Company for the ceremonial cup of tea. The entire Battalion is delighted.

In Pune, Raj learns that he has been awarded a Sena Medal for Bravery for an earlier action in J&K in which he shot two terrorists and captured one. He is told that the Battalion will try their best to retain him in service and depending on the rules, he will also be given full Disability Pension when he retires from service. In fact, his Commanding Officer ensures that Raj is given employment which does not aggravate his condition and yet gives him the satisfaction that he is very much an active participant in the Battalion's activities. In time, Raj is promoted to Havaldar and moves with his Battalion to Walong in Eastern Arunachal Pradesh. Here too, Raj makes himself an effective member of the Company and is, perhaps, the most popular NCO in the Battalion. The only point on which he differs from his colleagues and officers is about his marriage. He will not marry. Time marches on. After serving for 21 years in the Colours and finding himself deteriorating physically, Raj retires from service with a Service Pension-cum-Disability Pension which a paternal Government grant him for his lifelong services to the country and sacrifices without count, cheerfully given. He returns home via his Regimental Centre where the Centre Commandant asks him to stay on a few weeks more and motivate new recruits joining the Regiment. So Raj, the hero of this tale, returns home, having served his country with great distinction.

At the bus stand, his youngest brother is there to receive him, as are a few old friends. He walks home with only his hand bags while the black trunk (much travel scarred) and kit bag follows on a bullock cart. His mother weeps with joy as he reaches his home and makes him feel sorry that in the past 20 odd years, he spent only about 20 months with his dear mother. His father had passed away a few years earlier and the elder of the two younger brothers had joined the Artillery, four years after he himself had enlisted. So, he is the head of the family now and he will now look after his mother, younger brother, their plot of land, house and cattle. He will do this without anyone realising that he has only one leg, for he has learnt in the Army that 'one did what one had to – never mind the problems'. A new life begins for Raj.

He has many visitors initially. The local newspaper correspondent interviewes him and publishes a feature on him, photograph and all. The Collector of the District, on tour, visits his house to greet him and informs him that the State Government has sanctioned an ex-gratia payment of Rs. 100,000 on account of his having been disabled during active operations/counter-terrorist operations. He is touched because the Collector has personally come to his house to give him the cheque. And after this visit is reported in all the newspapers in the district, the local MLA, the aspiring MLAs and politicians of many different parties also come to meet him to try and persuade him to join their political party and to campaign for them in the forthcoming elections. Raj politely turns down all such invitations. He has learnt in the Army that a soldier should think deeply before deciding to join or not join politics. He has thought deeply and decided not to enter politics. Gradually, life regains its rhythm. He keeps himself busy all day, does everything he sets out to do, looks after his mother and his brothers and still has time to spend a happy evening with his friends. Thus, many years pass peacefully. One day, his mother, who had been suffering from cancer, dies in his arms.

Raj now makes it his mission to see that everyone in his village receives an early cancer check-up by a medical team whose annual visit he arranges. Similarly, he turns his attention to children's immunisation programmes, general standards of hygiene and sanitation and adult literacy programmes. He has become a social activist and people listen to him and follow what he says in letter and in spirit. They know he is a soldier and want nothing more than to be of service to the community.

When he reaches the age of 75 years, a team from his Regiment calls on him to present a Purse and a Ceremonial Shawl. He tells the young Major, the leader of the team that he is happy to meet such bright people from the Battalion and that he lacks nothing in life. He hosts a feast for the visitors and at the end of the meal, speaks a few words:

> "I joined the Army when I was 16 years of age. Since then, the Army has been my life and my soul. It gave me a full life, comradeship, action, adventurous life and a fair pay. It taught me all that I know and today, though I am retired and perhaps of no use to my Battalion, they still reach out to me. Someone once said that the Army took away my leg. No Sir, I lost a leg in action. But the Army has given me a new leg and whenever the new one becomes due for a change, the Army changes it with a brand new one! It has been a wonderful life, and thanks to the Army I want nothing more. Many people say that the Government should do this or that for me. Some of our own ex-servicemen's organisations (why do we have so many of them?) are constantly raising a clamour for more privileges, more facilities, etc. All I wish to say is that from the time I retired, till date, I have been given affection and respect by all sorts of people – Government officials, local body officials, politicians, fellow

citizens – everyone. If a soldier serves his country and returns to this kind of affectionate warmth and enjoys it for nearly 37-38 years, what else can he possibly want? If the people remember their soldiers in normal days and are friendly with them, that is about all that I think we need. I have nothing more to say except that if I die tomorrow and am reborn, I will again enlist into my old 'paltan'. Jai Hind."

Raj dies at dawn the next day, a satisfied smile on his face. His Regimental colleagues give him a funeral fit for royalty – such is the genuine love that they and the entire village evince towards him.

Such men as Raj are always remembered and cherished. For they are India's Soldiers.

11

The Media and Military

The term 'media' includes within its ambit all means of mass communication such as newspapers, magazines, radio, motion pictures, the wire services, television, the Internet and so on. Books, pamphlets/leaflets also fall under the heading of 'media'. The key determinants in judging whether an agency belongs to the genre of 'media' or not are:

- Is it being used to convey a message or information by a person or organisation?
- Is the recipient a mass of people rather than merely one or two or a few individuals?
- Is the method of sharing the information such that anyone can access that information with the appropriate tools?

By this test, 'media' will include print media, electronic media and the wire services. These could be either government owned or privately owned. Regardless of its ownership status, mass media exert a strong and often profound influence on the minds of recipients.

The military is often the subject of media attention – sometimes laudatory and sometimes critical. The reaction of military personnel to such coverage is born out of the realisation that countless others will also be receiving the same medium. A favourable mention pleases them whereas critical remarks make them unhappy. It really comes down to 'image', the manner in which people perceive the military. The military, like most professional bodies, is deeply concerned about its 'image', for it influences many things, ranging from individual self-esteem to collective elan; from recruitment strategies to the funding that the government may make in the next budget and so on.

Another attribute that makes 'media' profoundly influential is its ubiquitousness. Media pervades every nook and cranny of the world. It sees all and tells all. Even royalty is not spared the intrusive attention of the media as Her Majesty Queen Elizabeth II discovered for herself some years ago. Perhaps as a result of his unhappy experience with the media, Sir Johannes Bjelke-Petersen is reported to have said: "The greatest thing that could happen to the state and the nation is when we can get rid of all the media. Then we would live in peace and tranquillity, and no one would know anything". (*The Spectator*, 1987; extracted from Collins Concise Dictionary of Quotations). Though many of us may share Sir Johannes' desire, it is not likely to happen, ever; unless of course, humanity returns to the Stone Age because of some cataclysmic event. If anything, with ever improving communications and the remarkable manner in which computers and communications have converged, exponentially multiplying their individual capabilities, humanity has marvellous means of getting data, speech, pictures and now, even smells from across anywhere to anywhere. This truly is the Information Age, the Age of Mass Media.

In this chapter, we will discuss how the military should interact with the media so as to achieve positive coverage and enhance its image. We will first identify the salient characteristics of media and media persons; discuss what is 'news' and what events are 'newsworthy'; evolve some guidelines for interaction with media; and finally take note of the pitfalls that may exist in media-military interaction. Perhaps we should also include a few gratuitous pieces of advice to the media!

Characteristics of Media

Both print and electronic media have their own distinctive characteristics. While both deal with news, views, information and entertainment, the manner in which they present it to the reader or viewer is different. It will be helpful towards evolving our approach to interaction with media if we understand these characteristics. Likewise, media persons too are of various types and nature and, in their professional attitudes and actions, display a wide range of behaviour. It will be useful for our present purpose to study these as well.

Print Media: In India, the print media is, by and large, privately owned. The political beliefs and proclivities of the proprietors exercise profound effect on their editorial policy and even on the manner of coverage and analysis of news. Then, there are publications owned by political parties. These follow the party propaganda/information policy implicitly and being 'official' party organs, what appears in them is taken to be the party's view on that issue. However, whether a publication is ideologically slanted or not, its proprietors generally show considerable concern for the reputation of that publication in terms of truthfulness, speed and scope of what their publication carries. Some, of course, show even greater concern for the circulation figures and advertising revenues that their publications generate. So, all these considerations – political inclination, reputation of the publication, its circulation figures and the type of readers who read it, go towards determining how it deals with matters concerning the Armed Forces. Though proprietors do have a strong and even controlling influence on the publication's policies, except in the case of very small or niche publications, an Editorial Board consisting of senior heads of departments of the publication, is constituted to either formulate policy, or, to give effect to the dictates of the proprietor. By and large, the shape and nature of the publication, as it reaches the public, is determined by the Editorial Board. In India, government controlled print media are very few at both the national and state levels. These reflect the viewpoint of the government and do not enjoy wide circulation. Both privately owned and government controlled media derive considerable support from the government in the form of subsidy on newsprint, tax concessions on import of machinery and printing accessories and revenues from official advertisements. The newsprint subsidy and advertisement revenue, place in the hands of an unscrupulous government, a powerful tool to compel the media to toe their line. Fortunately, most governments have refrained from attempts to coerce the media and when any such attempt was made, the media has been able to withstand such pressures. The control of the government over print media is, therefore, much weaker than it was some decades ago. For all intents and purposes, India's print media is free and untrammeled by governmental influence.

Electronic Media: All India Radio and Doordarshan are wholly Government owned and reflect its views on affairs. Till a few years ago, it had a near monopoly on electronic media. However, the advent of commercial satellite television channels and the information explosion that occurred in the early 1990s, changed the situation radically. Today, television viewers have a plethora of national and international channels to choose from. With the introduction of digital set-top-boxes and direct-to-home transmissions, the quality of received telecasts too has improved significantly. Similarly, anyone with a short wave radio receiver can access news and other programmes from all over the world without difficulty. Notwithstanding all this, rural India in which 70 per cent of India's population lives, is still heavily dependent on Doordarshan and All India Radio, the economics of cable television and direct-to-home television systems being what it is. Despite these observations, electronic media has some important characteristics which make it more versatile and powerful than print media. These are:

- It has wider reach in real time.
- Higher frequency of broadcast/telecast.
- Audio/Audio-visual impact is greater.
- Listener/viewer has a greater sense of participation in the events covered.
- Tele-conference facility enables immediate listener/viewer response.
- Audience size at any one time is larger.
- The Internet and World Wide Web have brought to computer users virtually the entire knowledge bank of the world to their fingertips.

Wire Services: A word about wire services, which feed both print media and the newsrooms of electronic media. These are the equivalent of 'pool reporters' and sell their coverage of news to all their subscribers. Their power and reach are such that governments often give them special treatment. Reuters, Press Trust of India and AFP are a few wire services which readily come to mind. They are reporters and disseminators of news. But they will also carry what they consider could become news, often with a good chance of it being published. This is something we could keep in mind when handling media.

Media Persons: Media persons are truly the soul of media. They are professionals of varying calibres and types. They work to a very demanding schedule and are, therefore, often impatient and seemingly in a hurry. They tend to ask their questions directly and are often quite shocking in their bluntness. While most good media persons have the faculty of listening, quite a few tend to interrupt one frequently. Most of them are honest and diligent about their work. However, a few try to 'embellish' the truth or attempt to 'improve' a story by clever editing of one's statement or by so juxtaposing phrases used by one, as to convey an entirely different sense than what was intended to be conveyed. They are forever looking for 'one liners', 'quotes' and 'sound bytes' as something said tersely and in a succinct yet 'catchy' manner looks rather good in their story and gives it the ring of authenticity. A point we should keep in mind always is that for covering difficult assignments like in J&K or in Manipur, usually younger reporters are detailed by their papers/ channels. While youth has its own charm, one sees little of it in the 'cub' reporters who come to forward areas from the media. They are generally full of a sense of self-importance, sound brusque and brash, appear to be 'demanding' and often sound 'cheeky'. The opposite is true of the more elderly media persons. The point to note from all this talk about media persons is that they are exactly that – persons, with all the fads, foibles and idiosyncrasies from which none of us is free. And they have a job to do; often a deadline to meet. They seldom get the kind of logistic support we take for granted in the services and have to rough it out in poor accommodation, eat make-do meals, find transport for themselves, cope with crowded telephone outlets or lines which do not work. We need to make allowances for all this when we interact with them.

There are also some special categories of media persons. The specialised 'photo journalist' whose camera work speaks more eloquently than words ever can, the war correspondent who is to be found where there is a battle going on, either phoning in his 'story' via videophone or sending his dispatch in a more old fashioned manner, the 'disaster specialist' who reports so often from disaster areas that his very appearance on the television screen fills one with foreboding, sports correspondents, stock market specialists, parliamentary specialists and so many others who have made a name for themselves in their chosen fields. They are thorough professionals and carry out considerable background research before they go on their assignments.

Another category of media persons are those who have won fame by pioneering programmes like 'talk-shows', 'walk-the-talk' programmes, hard hitting interviews, public debates on television, psephologists with their election coverage, quiz masters, event commentators and so on. These specialists have lifted telecasts/broadcasts from the run-of-the-mill programmes, oriented more towards entertainment and transformed these into thought provoking and content-rich offerings which are of great interest to the listeners/viewers. All these media persons have great impact on their audiences. They help to focus attention on issues, subtly inject their own point of view and have a major role to play in forming or modifying public opinion.

No account of media or media persons will be complete without mention of two relatively recent developments in that field. First, the American concept of 'embedded' war correspondents, who, presumably will report favourably about the actions and inactions of their hosts whose miniature flag they wear on their jackets. The second is the craze (no other word can describe the phenomenon adequately) that has developed for public opinion surveys. In the Internet-SMS enabled world, it is certainly a temptation for the media to gain free publicity by running an opinion poll on some issue or the other and seeking SMS replies. If the issues are of some consequence, one could, perhaps accept this sort of polling; but, so many of the opinion poll subjects are so trivial that one feels foolish merely having the television set on at that time. So one switches off the set and lets the asinine poll give over to something more meaningful.

News and Newsworthiness

The military man often feels disappointed that some event, which he expected would be covered by both the print and the electronic media, is ignored. Perhaps the event was not 'news-worthy'. We need to understand what the terms 'news' and 'newsworthiness' mean to avoid such disappointments.

News is defined as 'information about recent events of general interest, specially as reported by the mass media'. This is a fairly restrictive definition. Today, news also includes anything from gossip and innuendo about persons, stories based upon partial information or even speculative stories. Not everything that is published is of general interest. Some items appeal to some people and some to others. Major affairs of state, great scientific or sporting achievements are generally of wider interest than, say, the inauguration of a library in a remote place. The modern principle for judging news-worthiness seems to be, "What sells is news". In our country, with so many of our national institutions showing signs of shakiness (if not actually crumbling), the Armed Forces are regarded by almost every Indian to be holding their own, amidst the general chaos. One would expect, therefore, that their activities would be of general interest and newsworthy by themselves. Unfortunately it is not the way the media sees it. To them, it would be news if a soldier runs amok and slays six others; it will be news if there is a civil-military melee at a railway station, leading to some casualties; it will be news if some sort of a lurid crime is committed by a military person. However, it may not rate high on the media's scale of newsworthiness if all that is on offer from the military is the 38th Raising Day of a unit. Perhaps one can take comfort from the old saying, "No news is good news". Or, is it? There can be no unqualified answer to this question. Let us take an example. Military Intelligence provided a major clue to Delhi Police a few years ago about some explosions that were engineered by terrorists in a busy market place, leading to the arrest of key members of the terrorist group that was responsible. Should this MI coup be splashed in all the print and electronic media, including photographs of a beaming Police Commissioner shaking hands with an officer from the MI? It will be good for the 'image' of the Army, no doubt. But, will it not compromise the identity of the MI officer and his freedom to operate in the Old Delhi area? In the event, we decided that it would and only a terse mention was made in the media stating that the MI assisted the Police in the case.

Let us go on now to frame a set of guidelines for the military's interaction with the media.

Guidelines for Interaction

Before we do anything else, we must resolve the conflict that exists between the requirement of the media for transparency and unfettered access to news and the traditional obsession with secrecy on the part of the military. Transparency and secrecy are diametrically opposing principles and bulk of the military's problems with the media arise because either they were inadequately communicative or were needlessly garrulous. A good way to resolve this issue is to ask oneself whether the information proposed to be shared with the media will be of advantage to the enemy or other interests hostile to us. If the answer is negative, the information may be freely shared. Of course, operational plans, deployments, movements, appreciation of the situation and matters relating to the morale of forces should be withheld from the media as long as their public disclosure will cause discomfiture to us.

Some simple guidelines for military personnel interacting with the media have been drawn up, as a result of experiences of a number of military media managers. These are likely to prove useful to both the military personnel as well as the media persons. The major points of guidance are:

- Treat media persons as professionals who have a difficult job to do. Treat them with courtesy and understanding. Do not be patronising or antagonistic.
- Listen to their questions carefully. Give out your replies crisply and clearly.
- Speak to them with well chosen words; the fewer the better! Avoid bombast as well as jargon. Go bilingual from time to time if you find some of the media persons are not following your language or diction clearly.

- Use maps, sketches, photographs and exhibits to assist everyone to follow the talk.
- Give out facts and figures as a 'handout'.
- Whenever a media person asks you for any comment 'off the record', remember that you should say only that which you would not mind seeing published in print or telecast.
- Do not try to bluff if you do not have the answer to a question. A frank, 'I do not know', will be the right thing to say.
- When a question calls for disclosure of classified material in reply, clearly tell the questioner that the matter is classified and you are not at liberty to speak about it.
- When questions call for your opinion on delicate matters on which you do not wish to speak, parry these with a terse 'No comment'.
- When dealing with unpleasant incidents on which media persons are asking you a barrage of questions, see that you have the facts of the case available to you. A clear statement giving the facts as known and proposed action will clear the air first. Do not indulge in any form of 'cover up'. Stick to facts.
- Rebut a wrong story immediately in clear and polite language.
- The media persons have deadliness to meet. Finish your meeting well in time and have them guided to a suitable place to file their story.

All these guidelines are quite straightforward and may appear to be 'basic'. Yet, how often have military men dealing with media in a field location 'come a cropper' because they violated something as 'basic' as what we have just listed! It may be better to follow these simple guidelines and by correct interaction with the media, win for the Armed Forces a useful friend and well meaning critic.

Some Pitfalls

Despite our best efforts to interact with the media in a transparent and unambiguously truthful manner, we may find ourselves in difficulties, some times. These are in the nature of pitfalls, much like the hazards on a golf course. If one plays carelessly or plays too close to the 'water hazard' or 'bunker', one may actually land up in one of these. So, it is with the pitfalls in our interaction with the media. Some of the common ones are listed below:

- Statements could be twisted out of shape altogether to convey an opposite meaning.

  We should communicate in unambiguous language to avoid this.

- Phrases could be so juxtaposed as to give a different message from what we intended.

  The watchword should be to say only what one means in clear, brief sentences.

- The story may be textually correct but the caption or headline could convey something entirely different.

  Caption writers are often different from the 'copy' writers. Issue a correction to rectify the damage.

- Classified information appears in the media.

  This is an in-house problem for the military to inquire into and resolve. Remember, media persons are not obliged to reveal their source of information.

- Individual services are specifically targeted in a number of issues, the entire publicity being adverse to the service and be likely to shake the people's faith in that institution.

  The reasons for this maybe many and none of these are worth discussing here. The best one can do is to meet the Chief Editor of the publication and suggest to him that the revelations/campaign against an institution like one of the services, has not served any media or national interest. Perhaps they will blame it all on a single correspondent but the message would have been received. They should be requested to publish a suitable correction to undo the damage already done.

A Few Suggestions to the Media

This chapter will not be complete until we inform the media of the expectations the services have from them. Stated briefly, these are:

- Be fair in your report. Remember, the Service cannot forever be sending rebuttals to an inaccurate story which has already done the damage! Check out the details with the Service concerned and in your haste to get a 'scoop', do not go off with a 'half-fact-half fiction' sort of a story.
- The Services are a major bastion of democracy. The people hold them in high regard. Therefore, in a report where you are referring to an 'one off' incident, do not criticise the entire Service. They are not at liberty on many occasions to defend themselves, though they have to defend the country all the time. They will be able to do this better if there is no 'sniping' from the media from the sidelines.
- Let your 'cubs' be 'blooded' under an experienced media person. Youth can commit rather serious mistakes in their inexperience and keenness.

- Not everything is meant for the public domain. A decent regard for individual privacy, as well as for the military units' sensitivities, should be observed.
- When reporting from an event-site, do keep in mind the tensions that local servicemen are under at that time. Do not aggravate matters by being too 'pressing'. It may be better if you give him a chance to calm down first!
- Sometimes a serviceman may unwittingly reveal some classified or other important matter the publication of which will adversely affect national security. If there is such a possibility, ask the person concerned again whether he wants his revelation to be published. And even if he says 'Yes', check with your Bureau Chief or senior whether it will not prejudice national security. Go by his advice.
- When working under active service conditions, be careful to observe all safety limits that your local Service Commander may have told you to observe. Implicitly follow any snap instructions, as your life and those of the troops you are working with, may depend on your action.
- Finally, remember your mission. Be sure you are accurate, timely, impartial and non-judgmental. The Services will esteem your work more, if you follow this advice.

Media needs to be accepted as an essential feature of modern life. It has a major role to play in moulding public opinion, adding to or diminishing one's image and, generally, in helping to 'shrink' the world community. The military must learn to interact with the media with confidence and in a transparent manner. To be able to do so, one has to understand the capabilities of the media, the manner in which the media persons function, the concept of news worthiness and observe such guidelines as are available. One should also be wary of the pitfalls, lest our aim in media-interaction be defeated. Military personnel need the media and must find ways and means to work harmoniously with media persons.

12

Is Peace Breaking Out in South Asia?

Asia is the largest continent on Planet Earth. Jutting out from this vast landmass and straddling the East-West trade routes is the promontory we call South Asia.

It is a large tract of land. Included in it are the countries that comprise the South Asian Association for Regional Cooperation (SAARC) – Bangladesh, Bhutan, India, Maldives, Nepal, Pakistan and Sri Lanka. These are not the most developed countries on Earth; quite the contrary. All of them are striving to improve the lot of their peoples so that they may lead fuller, healthier and happier lives. Seven developing countries, each with its hopes and aspirations, each with its own historical baggage and problems. They need peace for development. They need peace for breaking free from the shackles of ignorance, ill health, poverty and shortages of everything that matters. They need peace to become productive citizens of the human race and not merely remain as the most fecund group of peoples with the highest growth rate of population without corresponding growth of the wherewithal to sustain that population.

And, denying them the peace they sorely need, the seven countries are beset by numerous problems. The dogs of war rampage among some of them, tearing to shreds the thin pericardium-like membrane of peace that surrounds, protects and keeps strong the hearts of nations so that they may endeavour with greater gusto, greater energy. But war consumes their efforts – wars between countries, wars within countries, overt wars, covert wars and proxy wars. Can South Asia securely chain these feral canines? Can peace be preserved or re-created – not the fragile, china jar variety of peace that one stone thrown at it in anger can shatter, but a more robust kind of peace made of composite materials that combine resilience, strength and the ability to endure, even in the face of catastrophe, natural or man-made? Or, are we asking for the unattainable?

All of South Asia watches with bated breath as the 'battle' for peace rages. On the 'Centre Court' are India and Pakistan talking to each other after a long period of estrangement. To the north is the Himalayan kingdom of Nepal, in the throes of an agonizing struggle between the King and the Maoists, between monarchy and democracy. To the south is the beautiful emerald island of Sri Lanka, bruised and bleeding from over decades of internecine struggle with separatist Tamils, engaging them in peace talks facilitated by far off Norway. East of the SAARC region where the mighty Rivers Irrawady and Chindwin flow through forests and rich paddy fields, in Myanmar, military oligarchs rule the country while the 'elect' of democracy, her voice stifled, languishes, imprisoned in her own house. Between India and Myanmar lies Bangladesh, for now at peace but ready to go into turmoil if the forces of nature or the mutual incompatibilities of its two main political parties, will it to do so. Two small SAARC countries remain to be mentioned : The Himalayan kingdom of Bhutan, where an enlightened King has been able to preserve the peace against all odds and the island state of Maldives, of ethereal beauty, yet so low in the waters that it may be claimed by the ocean one day. This then is the South Asia family of nations, each member beset with its own problems or tangled in problems with its neighbours. And it is these very nations that are asking, "Is peace breaking out in South Asia?" – they and presumably the rest of the world. We will endeavour to answer this important question in this chapter.

In order to answer this question satisfactorily, we must understand what caused peace to play truant from South Asia generally and the sub-continent in particular. To do this, we need to delve into the history of these countries and then discover the roots of their problems. We will have to strip layer after layer of confusing overlays that cloud our perception of the real problems that plague us, much like ripping off the coir to expose the coconut and its shell, to get at the kernel. We will confine our study to India and Pakistan, as these two countries are currently engaged in a much talked about quest for peace. Though Sri Lanka's peace efforts predate those of India and Pakistan, we will have to omit them from this study for considerations of space. However, some references to Sri Lankan peace will be made in the closing stages of chapter.

The first advent of Arab Muslims into India is believed to have been around AD 637 when the great Chalukya King, Pulakesin II, ruled the north and western parts of the Deccan Peninsula from his capital at Vatapi. The event has been dated with reference to an 'army' sent to Thana near Bombay to evict the Arabs. Then onwards, they were drawn to India by the prospect of lucrative trade through ports from the Makran coast (now in Pakistan) to Kochi with what was then a rich and 'advanced' country. The Arabs acquired from the Hindus in Sind (conquered by AD 871) new knowledge about Indian religion, philosophy, medicine, mathematics, astronomy and folklore and took this not only to their own land but also exported it to Europe. From the 9th century onwards, there was a stream of Muslim invasions and conquests of India (fragmented as it was then) and the conversion of nearly a quarter of the Indian population (mainly Hindus and Buddhists) to Islam by 1858, when the British formally dissolved the Moghul empire.

Indian Muslims retained their distinctive identity. They established the Aligarh Muslim University in 1875 and founded the Muslim League in 1906. There was no movement for a separate Muslim homeland till 1930 when the great Punjabi poet Allama Mohammed Iqbal put out the idea. (Incidentally, Allama Iqbal also wrote the stirring song *'Sare jahan se achha, Hindustan hamara....'* (Our Hindustan is the most wonderful place in the whole world). At the Lahore session of the Muslim League its leader, Mr. Mohammed Ali Jinnah, declared his support for the idea of Pakistan. After prolonged and sometimes stormy negotiations, the Indian National Congress which was in the vanguard of the freedom movement conceded to the British that they accepted the partition of India and the creation of Pakistan. Pakistan was accordingly born on 14th August, 1947. Its territory included Baluchistan, Sind, North-West Frontier Province, West Punjab and East Bengal, the last two provinces coming to it after partition of undivided Punjab and Bengal of earlier days. J&K was invaded by Pakistan organised tribals and was nearly overrun by late October 1947, but the Maharaja of Kashmir, sought Indian military help to throw out the invaders and formally acceded to India on 27/28 October, 1947. By then, Pakistani troops had entered the fray openly and the fight between old comrades went on till the UN ordered a ceasefire with effect from 1st January, 1949. Since then, Pakistan has invaded the State three times (1965, 1971 and 1999) but has not achieved any success in terms of gaining territory. Its attempts to take control of the Siachen Glacier sector, taking advantage of vagueness in the delineation of the Line of Control in this sector, were also foiled by timely action of the Indian Army. This was in 1984.

Foiled in various attempts to capture more territory in J&K, Pakistan adopted for J&K, the ISI-CIA inspired strategy of 'death by a thousand cuts' which had succeeded in ousting the Najibullah Government in Afghanistan and had forced the Soviet troops to leave that country. Pakistan organised, armed, trained and launched into India, a large number of militants for fighting guerilla type actions in J&K against Indian security forces. The Indian reaction was initially weak and hesitant, but soon they saw through the Pakistani strategy in this 'proxy war' and got the better of them at every step. Far from collapsing under the weight of the proxy war, the people of J&K, in the best traditions of liberal democracies, went to the polls repeatedly to elect their own State Assembly, send representatives to the national Parliament in New Delhi and for local bodies within the State. All this should have convinced the protagonists of the 'Proxy War' that India was unlikely to yield to anything they tried for wresting J&K from it.

From 11th September, 2001 onwards, Pakistan, which by then was in a parlous economic and political state, became once again a front-line state and ally of the USA in their invasion of Afghanistan and the continuing 'search' for the elusive Osama bin Laden and his followers. At about the same time (13th December, 2001), a group of suicide bombers dispatched by a Pakistan controlled terrorist group, attacked the Indian Parliament. The terrorists were duly killed before they could cause any real damage but India's patience with Pakistan's abetment of cross-border terrorism had run out. Indian Armed Forces mobilised fully and were placed in what could only be read as offensive dispositions. With this, Pakistan's 'cup of misery', as it were, flowed over. It decided to accede to the US requests for air bases, passage facilitation for US ships and aircraft and full support including intelligence support to them against Afghanistan. What the USA promised Pakistan as '*quid pro quo*' can only be guessed. But the Indian forces did not attack, nor did Pakistan actually comply with Indian demands to stop cross-border terrorism and hand over some 'wanted' terrorists, etc. The USA for its part, got what they wanted – or at least appeared to have, as, though the Taliban regime has been removed, Osama seems to have 'vanished'. And so, with the USA re-charging its coffers and rescheduling the debts, giving it military equipment/spares and praising Pakistan's contributions to the USA's War against Terrorism, Pakistan continued with the proxy war against India in a 'business as usual' mode.

And, it was 'business as usual' too as India discovered on 14th May, 2002, when Pakistan trained and inspired terrorists attacked the Army's family quarters in Kaluchak (J&K) and killed 29 men, women and children in a barbaric act of terror. With Indian forces still deployed in forward positions and fighting rhetoric emanating from top Indian leaders, it seemed that war was imminent again. But with the USA by now heavily dependent on Pakistani support in its operations in Afghanistan, the Indians were counselled restraint and they duly obliged. Rather intriguingly, within one month of the Kaluchak massacre, India 'magnanimously' cleared overflights of India by Pakistani airliners, a ban that was enforced in December 2001 in the wake of the attack on the Indian Parliament! Strange are the ways of Indian politicians!

With no compliance from Pakistan of our demands, President Musharraf's telecast speech of 27th May, 2002, sounding more bellicose and intransigent than ever before, India's action in allowing overflights of our airspace by Pakistani aircraft is, to say the least, curious. Perhaps even then, peace-makers were busy behind the scenes, trying to cool Indian and Pakistani tempers, seeking common ground between the two countries so that they might begin to talk to each other about their problems. That is the best interpretation we can put on the Indian relaxation of the ban on overflights by Pakistan.

The situation in J&K dragged on through the years 2002 and 2003 with no evidence of Pakistan stopping her proxy war, nor of India slackening its anti-terrorist actions. The macabre dance of death continued in J&K with many terrorists, security forces personnel and innocents perishing while Pakistan persisted with its unwinnable proxy war and India continued its anti-terrorist operations with increased vigour. And then something happened.

In November 2003, a ceasefire agreement was concluded by India and Pakistan to cover the entire Line of Control Sector as well as the Glacier Sector. A summit meeting between India and Pakistan took place at Islamabad on 5th January, 2004, on the sidelines of the SAARC summit. It gave further impetus to the peace process. The composite dialogue framework that was evolved in 1999, was revived and both sides reiterated their sincerity in wishing to discuss all issues between India and Pakistan, including the 'core' issue of Kashmir, as Pakistan's President Musharraf had made amply clear by countless reiterations.

But perhaps, we should go back to the bus ride which the then Indian Prime Minister Atal Behari Vajpayee took to Lahore in 1999, as the opening bar in a major overture for peace. There was general acclaim for the move and hope for peace was strong. There were, however, some wrong chords struck that were noticeable : General Musharaff, the Pakistan Army Chief, was not present at the initial line up to receive the Indian Prime Minister. By itself, it amounted to no worse than a display of petty pique, but taken as an expression of the Pakistan Army's general aversion to Prime Ministers – be they Pakistani or Indian – it did suggest that there were reservations about the peace moves among Pakistan's uniformed fraternity. Or, maybe, even then, the knives were being sharpened for the Kargil 'back-stab' in the summer of 1999 and the General, as an honourable man, could not bring himself to participate in a charade, a public fraud, which is what the 1999 peace process became.

The welcome given by the people of 'Nehar Wali Haveli' of Delhi to their illustrious former resident General Pervez Musharraf en route to the Agra Summit on 14th July, 2001, seemed euphoric but it was euphoria minus a sense of confidence that what followed would be equally pleasant. Well, it was not. General Musharraf, in retrospect, could be accused of 'grandstanding' in Agra. He built up his image and belittled the Indian political hierarchy by implication, if not directly. His breakfast meet with the press certainly broke something – it broke the very spirit of the summit. All South Asia was disappointed at the outcome and in India, there was suppressed anger that General Musharraf showed such poor manners towards a person like the Indian Prime Minister, who, though 'stabbed' in the back' in 1999, still called the General over for summit parleys in order to establish peace in the sub-continent; a gentleman certainly, though not a military officer like General Musharraf.

And in November 2003, less than three years later, the same gentleman, Mr. Vajpayee, seeing a ray of hope in the overall situation involving the sub-continent, the USA and the stable conditions in J&K, declared an unilateral ceasefire, all over J&K's borders. Pakistan accepted the ceasefire and since then till now, barring a few minor violations, there has been a genuine ceasefire on the Indo-Pak frontiers. Even in the frozen wastes of the Saltoro Ridge, the guns have fallen silent. The number of civilian and military casualties on the borders has plummetted to nothing. However, terrorists are still active in J&K and anti-terrorist actions are still going on.

The January 2004 summit, we referred to earlier, was thus, held in an atmosphere relatively un-polluted by gun smoke and was productive. The joint statement stated that they had agreed to resume the composite dialogue which, they asserted, "would lead to the peaceful settlement of all bilateral issues including Jammu and Kashmir to the satisfaction of both sides". President Musharraf had reassured Prime Minister Vajpayee that "he would not permit any territory under Pakistan's control to be used to support terrorism in any manner". This was progress indeed. Barring the militant groups closely linked to the Pakistan Army (Hizbul Mujahideen and Jamait-ul-Mujahideen), the joint statement was welcomed by India and Pakistan. There seemed to have occurred a progressive change in the Indo-Pak situation since the grim days of 2002, when the armies of India and Pakistan were deployed for war against each other for 10 months. What caused this change has been the subject of speculation among political commentators, journalists and the people of both India and Pakistan. All of them felt that something, which was not yet available in the public domain, had exercised a benign influence on the leaders of both countries, but what this 'mysterious' event was, is not known. We believe that the change of heart in both India and Pakistan, since the end of 2002, was on account of the following reasons:

- India and Pakistan, two neo-nuclear states, came very close to fighting a war with each other. Such a war would have seriously retarded the USA's 'War on Terrorism', as Pakistan's forces cooperating with the Americans would have to redeploy for war against India and would not be available to the US. This being counter to its interests, would have been prevented by the USA.
- The 2002 'near war' could have escalated from conventional to nuclear war, specially, as India's immensely superior strategic situation would have reduced Pakistan to an unacceptably disadvantageous or even an extremely precarious position, forcing it to threaten the use of nuclear weapons or actually use them. This would have triggered an Indian retalliation, leading to horrendous casualties on both sides and collaterally on the forces of the USA and its other allies in Pakistan. Once the nuclear 'genie' was released from the 'bottle', it would be very difficult to regain control of the situation by either the belligerents or the superpower. Such a prospect must never be allowed to rise and the USA would no doubt have employed every diplomatic, economic and punitive means at its disposal to eliminate the possibility of a war between India and Pakistan.
- The ceasefire which took effect in November 2003, was observed by both sides with commendable sincerity, barring a few minor violations. But this was not a new phenomenon, as far as troops of the two countries are concerned. There was an

earlier 'informal' ceasefire in 2000-2001, concurrent with a formal abjuration of offensive operations by security forces against the militant groups. Then too, there was an effective ceasefire on the LOC. But this 'ceasefire' differed from that of 2003, on some significant points. Firstly, it was 'informal' and did not include the Siachen Glacier sector. Secondly, though the security forces had unilaterally declared a ceasefire against the militants, the militants continued their depredations against the people of J&K. Their camps across the LOC were still trying to pump into India, trained batches of militants who had been awaiting infiltration in various camps close to the LOC in Occupied Kashmir. Thus, though in the 2000-2001 ceasefire too, casualties on and close to LOC were reduced, in the interior, fighting continued leading to casualties among militants, security forces and the common people. A climate conducive to talks did not exist at any stage in the period from the Agra Summit in July 2001 till about October 2003 by which time the combined effect of the ceasefire and a whole range of confidence building measures had helped convince both sides that they could now trust each other enough, to resume peace talks.

- A great deal of 'shuttle diplomacy' by the USA and others helped to bridge the gap in communications between the two countries. Also, working behind the scenes were many concerned citizens of both countries who travelled to and fro, meeting the leaders of both sides as well as the common people, trying to promote mutual trust, goodwill and a desire to arrive at a lasting solution to the problems that have bedevilled relations between India and Pakistan for so long.

- There were also 'back channel' meetings over a number of months, at various places outside the two India and Pakistan, between senior officials of the two countries, for the specific purpose of preparing the ground for talks and formulating possible articles of agreement at the end of these talks.
- Internal threats from Islamic extremists had reached alarming levels. In December 2003 alone, two attempts were made on the life of the Pakistani President. The 'Jehadi' ultras accused President Musharraf of having 'sold out' on the Taliban to the USA and were now alleging a similar 'sell out' of Kashmiri interests to India. President Musharraf decided to take these ultras 'head on' as it were and persist on the course of action he had determined to be in the interest of his country. In India too, there was a clear realization that without President Musharraf being at the helm of affairs in Pakistan, no agreement could be arrived at with them, as there was no other leader in Pakistan who could take substantive decisions on Indo-Pak affairs despite the opposition of the 'Jehadis' and ensure that the Army in Pakistan accepted his decisions. India's earlier position that they could not negotiate with a 'dictator' also got resolved with the installation of an elected Government in Pakistan.

Thus, it would appear that the 5th January, 2004, summit meeting between India and Pakistan at Islamabad took place under very propitious conditions in India (including J&K) and Pakistan. It clearly had all the ingredients that make for success in such matters. Above all, the people of India and Pakistan, as well as the people of J&K on both sides of the Line of Control, were tired of the constant tension between the two neighbours. This tension has affected our lives in every possible way – from national security to playing cricket matches, from our economies to our performing arts – you name any field of human endeavour and the oppressive Indo-Pak tension had given it a skew, distorted it and made it unattainable or unenjoyable. The relations between our two countries have so far been an example of how two neighbouring countries should not behave with each other. Perhaps the 5th January, 2004, summit has set afoot new dynamics which will gather momentum, despite change of Government in India and take both countries into an era of peace. That is what we hope for : let us assess how much of our hopes can be realised.

Some important milestones in Indo-Pak relations and a short assessment of the extent to which they achieved the desired results, will be revealing:

- **1972- Shimla Accord:** Principle of bilateralism was accepted by both countries. Pakistan has constantly tried to renege on bilateralism and sought third party or UN intervention to resolve the J&K issue. India harps on the Shimla Accord. The result so far : nil.
- **February 1999- Lahore Declaration:** Amidst great bonhomie, the two sides agreed to enter into a composite dialogue process to discuss not only J&K issue but also economic, trade and other matters. Before the ink was dry on the Declaration, Pakistan committed armed aggression in the Kargil sector and had to be evicted after a bitter fight. The result of the Lahore Declaration : nil.
- **July 2001- Agra Summit:** It was undertaken without adequate preparation from our side and for startlingly different motives than achieving durable peace by Pakistan. Result : disaster for mutual trust; otherwise : nil.

- **12th January 2002- Speech of General Musharraf:** General Musharraf in his televised speech, probably as a result of US pressure to keep India 'off the boil', declared that Pakistan will not allow its territory to be used for terrorist activities. Outcome: only 'cosmetic' control of cross-border terrorism was carried out for general consumption. Actual result : nil.

The record for the past 30 years is certainly dismal. It shows that to Pakistan, the Accord/Declaration/ Statement, were strategic ploys meant to get Pakistan out of an awkward strategic situation. The Shimla Accord secured the repatriation of Pakistani prisoners of war held by us (over 80,000 personnel) at the cost of committing themself to the principle of bilateralism. They later hanged the man who signed the Accord and have spared no effort to make the Accord too, a dead letter. The Lahore Declaration was a charade as it appears now. Pakistan had already fully planned the Kargil aggression and was actually in the process of implementing it when the Lahore Declaration was hailed as a step towards peace. The Pakistan Army (specially General Musharraf, who was COAS then and is COAS and President now) had clearly accepted the then Prime Minister Nawaz Sharief's Lahore formulations as a good cover plan for keeping their Kargil plans under wraps. The Agra Summit, where a media coup of sorts was achieved by the Pakistani President, was designed to build up his image as the tough new leader of Pakistan who could put the 'soft' Indian leaders in their place by his forthrightness (boorishness?), media friendliness (exploiting India's media?) and charisma (even the late Z.A. Bhutto possessed charisma!). As for the 12th January, 2002 televised speech, it was a desperate attempt to tide over a very difficult strategic situation with the Indian Army massed on the border, the Americans

pressurising him to 'accommodate the Indians' so that he may support the American War on Terror better and the religious extremists and the 'rump' opposition parties accusing him of selling out to the Americans to save his own position. The General achieved his aim; neither India nor the USA achieved their aims! And so, we are again face to face with yet another milestone in India-Pakistan relations – the Islamabad Declaration of 6th January, 2004. Is it yet another piece of specious posturing, a piece of consummate deviousness or is it a genuine expression of Pakistan's desire for rapprochement with its neighbour, India? Let us address these questions now.

Qualitatively, the Shimla Accord was in a class of its own. It was an accord signed between two elected leaders of India and Pakistan. The victor, India, was if anything, magnanimous to a fault. All that India achieved were Pakistan's acceptance of the principle of bilateralism and the sanctity of the Line of Control. Pakistan got back a huge number of prisoners of war and a far better deal than they or anyone else expected. We too have, of course, heard of verbal agreements/ separate agreements in relation to the Line of Control being accepted as the international border in J&K, but these are mere rumours and unverifiable, as the principal parties concerned, have passed on. So, we will not further discuss the Shimla Accord, though it is valid, addresses India's concerns and is binding on both parties.

The Lahore Declaration, the Agra Summit and the 12th January, 2002, speech of General Musharraf, were all of a piece, being part of Pakistan's self-serving strategy, having little to do with the spirit of bilateralism or the establishment of durable peace and good neighbourly relations on the sub-continent. A notable common factor in all these events was that India was led by Mr. Atal

Behari Vajpayee who was repeatedly disappointed at the manner in which Pakistan would not allow his deep and sincere attempts to usher in peace to the sub-continent to succeed; and it is to his credit and persistent quest for peace that the current peace process owes its origin.

The train of events, as they occurred since the fighting in Kargil (1999) were:

- Vigorous activity on the part of non-official groups, functioning with Government's approval, to identify common ground between India and Pakistan on which they could base future peace talks, had been going on even before 1999. These were intensified after the Kargil Operations. These groups met most of the leaders who mattered in Pakistan (including their President) more than once and on return, fully briefed the Government on their visits. About this time, 'back channel' diplomacy also started and at a very high level. Their inputs, those of the non-official 'Track 2' and the Ministry of External Affairs' channels, all combined to give the Prime Minister a clear understanding of the prospects for initiating a peace process with Pakistan. Perhaps these inputs were not available or as refined in content as they seem to have become later, at the time of the ill-fated Agra Summit. However, the Government was unflagging in its quest for peace though on the Pakistani side, there was an equally unflagging effort to de-stabilise India through perpetuation of cross-border terrorism.
- Then came '9-11' and in the aftermath of that dastardly crime against humanity, the USA arrived in our neighbourhood, seeking to make 'War on Terrorism' along with its allies. Pakistan was an unwilling volunteer to start with as it was the one

who was the first to recognise the Taliban regime in Afghanistan, fund them, help them with military hardware, training and so on, in return for what they had been seeking to achieve since their birth – Strategic Depth. As events transpired, they were left with no choice in the matter by the USA and so they abandoned the Taliban after securing from the former a promise (later fulfilled) to allow them to extricate the 1000 plus officers and men of the Pakistan Army, still in beleaguered Afghanistan, when 'Operation Enduring Freedom' commenced. Necessity and expediency make for strange 'bedfellows'! How else can we view the alliance of the arch 'crusader' against terrorism and the 'high priest' of terrorism in South Asia? Be that as it may, perhaps as a result of wrong reading of the depth of Pakistan's desire for peace talks or through persuasion by the US and British officials who seemed to be 'forever' visiting Pakistan and India, India invited Pakistan for a summit meeting at Agra in July 2001. The summit was duly held and that was about the only positive feature of that very forgettable event. And so, through summer and the monsoons, the US and its allies including Pakistan, 'fought' terrorism in Afghanistan, while Pakistan continued its proxy war against India in Jammu and Kashmir.

- The '9-11' event seems to have encouraged the terrorist groups, directly controlled by Pakistan's ISI. On 1st October, 2001, the Jammu & Kashmir Assembly in Srinagar was attacked. 'Soft' targets in J&K were repeatedly hit by terrorists. And on 13th December, 2001, the Indian Parliament was attacked by a suicide squad. India mobilised and deployed its armed forces for war. On 12th January, 2002, clearly as a result of energetic persuasion by a thoroughly alarmed USA, General Musharraf made a speech in which he promised to ensure that Pakistani territory was not allowed to be used for terrorist activities. India maintained its deployment on the border but allowed itself to be mollified and not resort to military operations against the terrorists and their masters. The moment for action passed but, despite his assurances, there seemed to be no decrease in cross-border terrorism. Another grievous provocation was given to India on 14th May, 2002, when in a bestial action, 29 members of the families of Army personnel, in the small military station of Kalu Chak, were massacred by terrorists. They too came from Pakistan as did General Musharraf's expression of sympathy. How cynical can one get! Again, India allowed itself to be persuaded by its new neighbour from going to war and another crime against our citizens went unpunished; a sorry tale, often repeated in our context. But more surprises were in store for the country.

- In June 2002, the very next month after the Kalu Chak killings, even as the Armed Forces were in a state of operational deployment, the Government, in pursuance of some strange logic, commenced the process of easing up on its sanctions against Pakistan, starting with removing the ban on overflights over India. It seemed that the streams of visitors from the USA and the return visits from our side, all through the first half of 2002, had achieved their purpose. It seemed that India had been effectively prevented from making its own foreign policy decisions with respect to Pakistan, as it would run counter to the desire of our 'new neighbour', the USA! It took till 16th October, 2002, to release the Army from forward deployment.

- The winter of 2002/2003 saw cross-border infiltration reach a seasonal low. Track 2 and back channel activity reached a high level and continued in this vein all through 2003 and 2004. Diplomatic activity also became intense, with South Block, clearly sensing a closer Indo-US relationship developing, making every effort to develop a strategic partnership with the USA which would ensure that our views would always be sought in world affairs and the Armed Forces and Defence Ministries would enjoy a closer relationship with their American counterparts. All that actually came to pass in 2003-2004. But in April 2003, though the contours of an emerging Indo-US strategic relationship were becoming clear, there was really no apparent change in Pakistan's sponsorship of the proxy war against us nor of the activities of terrorist groups in J&K. True, the operations of security forces all through the winter of 2002/03 had played havoc with the leadership and logistics of these terrorist groups and their morale was at a very low point, not quite the nadir yet, but low enough for the then Prime Minister to again offer Pakistan, India's hand of friendship, during his visit to Srinagar on 18th April, 2003. The response from Pakistan was gratifying. The then Prime Minister of Pakistan, Mr. Zafarullah Khan Jamali, spoke to Mr. Vajpayee on 28th April, 2003, expressing his high appreciation of the Indian initiative and offering his full cooperation in the matter of rebuilding the India-Pakistan relationship on the basis of good neighbourliness and peace. He also invited Mr. Vajpayee to visit Islamabad. This exchange between the Prime Ministers set the tone for the rest of 2003. The restoration of full diplomatic ties with Pakistan was announced by

Mr. Vajpayee in Parliament on 3rd May, 2003. Within hours, Pakistan declared that it would respond in like manner. Mr Vajpayee, in his address to the Parliament said, "We are committed to the improvement of relations with Pakistan and are willing to grasp every opportunity for doing so".

- However, Mr. Vajpayee also stated that there would be no question of a 'third party' mediation between the two neighbours nor had India given up its demand for Pakistan to stop aiding and abetting cross-border terrorism. He stated, "We have repeatedly expressed the need to create a conducive atmosphere for a sustained dialogue which necessarily requires an end to cross-border terrorism and the dismantling of its infrastructure". He also said in a somewhat sentimental vein that this attempt would be the third he was making to settle differences with Pakistan and "will be decisive and the last in his lifetime". The atmospherics for the third attempt seemed just right. There was very little anti-India propaganda in official media and barring a few 'die-hards', even the traditional India-baiters among the Pakistani media, held their peace and did not run down Mr. Vajpayee's peace initiative. Both countries, clearly were in a mood to talk 'peace'.
- By October 2003, a number of confidence building measures were mooted. The Muzaffarabad-Srinagar Bus Service was one such. (The service has since started.) A very large number of people-to-people contacts, of legislators, professionals and businessmen took place. In November 2003, India declared an unilateral ceasefire all along the Indo-Pak border, Line of Control and the Actual Ground Position Line (AGPL) in the Glacier Sector. Pakistan fully reciprocated and the military of both sides

tied up a number of practical details to see that the ceasefire was properly observed and to resolve any problems that may arise in its implementation. In mid-December 2003, President Musharraf gave a strong indication that Pakistan intended to be flexible in future peace talks. In an interview with Reuters, President Musharraf stated that he was willing to put the UN Security Council resolutions on Kashmir (inter alia, calling for a plebiscite to determine the future of the state) on the back burner and talk of other ways to resolve the Kashmir issue. Despite attempts to assassinate him soon after this, he did not resile from his new position. All this was good augury and the stage was set for the meeting of the two leaders at the SAARC Summit at Islamabad in January 2004.

- We have already stated that the 'personal' summit between President Musharraf and Mr. Vajpayee, was a great success. Their joint statement committed the two countries to holding a 'composite dialogue' and not to let any one issue prevent forward movement in other areas. Soon after the summit, a series of official level talks started and even as India went to the polls, preparations were going on for an early meeting at ministerial level.

- The General Election results were declared on 13th May, 2004. The incumbent National Democratic Alliance government was voted out. Instead, on 19th May, 2004, the President of India invited Dr. Manmohan Singh to form the Government of a new coalition of parties, 'United Progressive Alliance' (UPA), led by the Indian National Congress. The question that many countries asked and a large number of people in India and Pakistan worried about was what would become of the peace process. But they need not have worried as events turned out.

- Mr. Natwar Singh, an experienced former External Affairs Minister, once again took over that portfolio and soon, he and his Pakistani counterpart, Mr. Khurshid Mahmud Kasuri, met in Qingdoo, China, on the sidelines of a regional conference. Here Mr. Natwar Singh assured Mr. Kasuri that India remained committed to the path of dialogue to solve all bilateral issues. Coming as this reassurance did after the June 27-28, 2004, Foreign Secretary level talks in New Delhi, it was good augury for the future of the peace process. It was as though the change of Governments in India had not significantly impacted the peace process, except for the reference to the UN Charter and the Shimla Agreement in the joint statement issued after the Foreign Secretaries talks in late June 2004.

- There has been progress on many issues, nothing spectacular, but progress of the steady, purposeful kind. Expert level talks were held on June 19th and 20th, 2004, on Confidence Building Measures (CBMs) and on nuclear weapons at New Delhi. Follow up action on various connected issues and on Kashmir centred CBMs is in progress. There has been a thinning out of troops from J&K by India, the numbers being estimated at the equivalent of two brigades. The survey of the ambiguously demarcated border along Sir Creek in the Kutch area, has started as agreed upon by the two Foreign Ministers in New Delhi in September 2004. The settlement of the entire Sir Creek issue, including delimiting the Sir Creek (it shifts) and the maritime boundaries with their effect on the Exclusive Economic Zones (EEZ) of the two countries, is likely to take a considerable amount of time. Nevertheless, the fact that a dispute is being attacked with the intellect and technology rather than by force, gives one reason to hope that it will eventually be resolved.

- The Baglihar Dam issue in which Pakistan has contended that the dam contravenes the Indus Water Treaty of 1960, under which Pakistan would enjoy exclusively the waters of the Indus, the Jhelum and the Chenab Rivers, barring some nominal outages, was discussed by experts on both sides. India defended its design and ongoing construction of the Rs 4500 crore, 450 Megawatt project, due to be completed in 2007, stating that it is a 'run-of-the-river' project and is covered by the Indus Waters Treaty, 1960. The matter was referred by Pakistan to the World Bank for the views of neutral experts. It looks likely that the matter may have to be referred to Arbitrators. One hopes that the issue does not become a 'casus belli' between the two countries as per the scenario depicted by this author in his book '*The Writing on The Wall – India Takes on the USA, 2017*'. It is not unlikely that India will adopt a 'harder' position on this project, seeing how the 'Wullar Barrage/Tulbul Navigation Project' has been blocked by Pakistan for many years now, using the same tactics as in the case of the Baglihar Dam. Pakistan fears that India would be able to 'dry up' the areas watered by the River Chenab in their part of Punjab or 'flood' it as the case may be. India feels that Pakistan's paranoid fears are blocking economic development of J&K. More than merely solving the engineering conundrum, therefore, the two nations must address the problem of mutual distrust between the countries. Peace cannot be based on suspicion – that state of mind is more likely to lead to conflict.

- Other subjects of the composite dialogue like Siachen, terrorism and drug trafficking, economic and commercial cooperation and promotion of friendly exchanges in various fields have come in for initial discussions. The Foreign Ministers have met a number of times. It was through such visits that the two Foreign Ministers and their teams of officials gave final shape to the Muzaffarabad-Srinagar Bus Service, whose inaugural run on 7th April, 2005, was not just a 'television event' but an excellent beginning to the process of bringing together the people on either side of the Line of Control. The linking of Sind and Rajasthan by road/broad gauge railway is now to be achieved by 01 January, 2006, while the suggested ferry service between Karachi and Mumbai may take longer. Despite pessimism in some quarters, we are convinced that these projects which bring the people of the two countries together, are the best form of insurance against re-estrangement or worse. Perhaps, their value in money terms may be far less than the gas pipeline from the CARs/Iran through Pakistan to India, but their 'peace dividend' is likely to be greater. On the same line of reasoning, the World Punjabi Conference (1st December, 2004) and the First Indo-Pak Punjab Games (5th to 11th December, 2004), though restricted to two subunits of our countries, have, nevertheless contributed greatly to the peace process by improving the overall atmospherics in both countries; so it was with cricket and the Indian tour of Pakistan in 2004. Pakistani's tour of India in March-April 2005, has also been as significant. The well-publicised medical treatment of Pakistani infants in India's leading hospitals in the South during 2003-2004, has also contributed to building bridges of friendship with our neighbour, long estranged.

The most significant event in Indo-Pak relations in the recent past was the visit of President Musharraf and a large entourage to Ajmer and Delhi in April 2005. Despite all kinds of apprehensions in many people's minds, regarding the success of this visit, it was a complete success. The fact that a joint statement was issued after the Summit meetings and that President Musharraf and Prime Minister Manmohan Singh established good personal rapport augurs well for the Indo-Pak peace process.

Lest we are accused of taking an over optimistic view and ignoring real obstacles to peace that exist, we will list these below:

- **Historical 'Baggage':** Through long years of strained relations, a sizeable stock of unpleasant experiences with each other has built up. This baggage is used to provide a 'frame of reference' or 'precedent', whenever either side is considering a developing situation or a course of action. The politicians and policy makers, servicemen and bureaucrats, professionals and the general public, having been conditioned by past experiences to think negatively about the other country and its motives, generally incline towards viewing any proposal or action initiated by the other country with cynicism and deep distrust. This 'baggage' needs to be jettisoned if progress is to be made in the peace process.

- **National Interests:** The J&K issue has been a rallying point for Pakistan. Whenever a civilian government was tottering, the issue was used to divert people's attention and obfuscate the real state of the country. Military regimes often trotted out the magic phrase, "The Unfinished Business of the Partition", as though to legitimise their taking over the reins of the country. Likewise, India, with a secular state structure and more Muslims among its population than Pakistan's entire population, has a deep and abiding interest in ensuring that the only Muslim majority state in India does not secede from the Union or join Pakistan in any manner. India feels that such an occurrence will undermine the foundation of India as a multi-religious, secular country and lead to its 'balkanisation'. Both countries, therefore, want J&K – not for its territory as they always say, but because it involves two conflicting concepts – that of religion and secularism and whether a country formed on the basis of religion has a claim on co-religionists in the neighbouring secular country and the impact it will have on the secular country's credibility if it permits the religious minorities to join its religious neighbouring state. There are no easy solutions to this problem; hence, the pessimism of the debunkers of the peace process about its success since the 'core' issue would not be resolved.

- **Class Interests:** A number of political analysts believe that perpetuation of the Kashmir issue is necessary for the Pakistan Army, Pakistani clergy and the terrorist groups, together with their puppeteers in the ISI. An army without an enemy will soon be out of work and may be downsized as well as downgraded in terms of its political relevance. The clergy who find gainful employment and a perverse sense of fulfillment by filling the terrorist trainees with 'jehadi' poison, will also become redundant. The terrorist groups will wither for want of state funding or collections through religious institutions, the ISI and from criminal connections and to survive will take to crime in a big way. Pakistan will become a country overrun by ex-terrorists now turned criminals, if there is peace with India and the J&K issue is resolved. We saw the same ugly phenomenon occur when the Soviets pulled out of Afghanistan and the Najibullah regime was replaced by the Taliban. The out-of-work terrorists were exported under the aegis of the ISI to J&K, Chechnya and a lesser number to reinforce the Uighurs in the Urumchi area of China. It would not be surprising, therefore, that with peace restored with India, the terrorists may turn on the 'hand that fed them', Pakistan. And finally, the ISI: its *raison d'etre* is the promotion of instability and chaos in its target areas through subversion, sabotage and violent anti-state activities. They will be out of business if they are warned off India by their national government. With all these 'class' interests likely to be adversely affected by establishment of peace with India, these analysts reckon that Pakistan may engage us in talks that lead nowhere and eventually peter out like all previous talks have done.

- **Nature of Indo-Pak Problems:** There are some who have articulated the view that as long as Pakistan exists, there will be a Kashmir problem. We need not let such extreme ideas detain us; they were probably uttered out of sheer frustration at not being able to find a solution to the Kashmir issue. Other Indo-Pak problems too are intricate and need both goodwill and statesmanship to resolve. For nearly 17 years, the Tulbul project languishes because of Pakistan's blocking tactics. Now, the same tactics are sought to be repeated in the case of Baglihar. The Sir Creek surveys and eventual settlement of the maritime boundary, entailing as it does, loss or gain of hundreds of thousand square kilometres of Exclusive Economic Zone will pose equally serious difficulties. Why – even the relatively small matter of opening Consulates in some of our cities like Karachi and Mumbai seems to be a major problem! In fact, Indo-Pak problems may be, in reality, capable of rational solutions. However, with the enormous overlays that both countries have laid over these problems – overlays of mistrust, hatred, deceit and periodic blood-baths — the solutions that are rational, appear to have sinister aspects and are never accepted by either side. The Siachen talks of a little over a decade ago and which, reportedly, had reached the point of conflict resolution, overnight broke into fresh wrangling! Something similar is believed to have happened in Agra in 2001. Indo-Pak problems have become so tied up with 'other' issues that they seem to be insoluble. And, if that is so, how can the peace process lead anywhere but to disappointment?

- **Misperceptions:** India is perceived as a 'soft' Hindu majority state in which Muslims are treated as second class citizens and periodically subjected to 'pogroms', reminiscent of Nazi Germany's against Jewish people. India is believed to be constantly planning the undoing of Pakistan, as the events of 1971 showed. Some 'India Specialists' in Pakistan believe that India will break up sooner or later under the weight of its religious, racial, linguistic and cultural differences and that the separatist movements of the North-East and J&K are precursors to this eventuality. Clearly, one may ask, why should Pakistan make peace with a floundering state rather than give India a vigorous push and end its misery? Indians too have their perceptions of Pakistan, some of which we believe are true while some are not. It is true that Pakistan has been the source of terrorism in South Asia and that its hyper-active intelligence agency, the ISI, has been meddling in our affairs continuously. We believe that Pakistan has permanently lost the 'ways' of democracy and will generally be a military dictatorship with caprices derived from the Dictator. It would be prudent to remain on guard against such an unpredictable state. Some in India hold that Pakistan is a religious state, that it is teetering on the brink of 'failing' and that it cannot but break up into fragments sooner or later! We fear the bloodshed attendant on the Partition and the wars between our two countries have so distorted our perceptions about each other that one does not find it easy to distinguish between honest beliefs and self-delusions; between reality and wishful thinking. It was the late, unlamented Herr Goebbels, who is believed to have said that a lie oft repeated soon becomes the 'truth'. And, so it seems, has been the case in Indo-Pak relations. Both countries have fallen victim to their own delusions and misperceptions. Unless these are cleared from our minds and the two countries interact in an honest and trusting manner, the peace process is likely to fail.

- **Hostile Propaganda:** Just as the 'senior league' players – the two Power Blocs—did during the Cold War, India and Pakistan have directed a stream of propaganda against each other. The atmosphere thus created was insufferably unhealthy. The media ran riot and the average citizen was convinced that he lived in the neighbourhood of a country that was evil personified and bore nothing but ill will towards his country. Such are the effects of persistent

> propaganda! With the advent of television and easier access to a large number of unbiased channels, people on both sides of the border are beginning to see through the propaganda and get a reasonably clear idea of ground realities in the sub-continent. Perhaps, that is one of the reasons for the increasing warmth the people of Pakistan and India have been displaying towards each other in the recent past. However, there are a lot of people who do not wish to believe the reality. Truly, there is no one more deaf than one who refuses to hear, nor more blind than one who refuses to see! The shutting off of the propaganda 'mills' will be a great step towards giving the peace process a chance to succeed.

From this litany of factors that are likely to prevent the peace process succeeding in its aims, it would appear that the prospects of success are bleak. So far, we have not seen unmistakable evidence of Pakistan rolling back its proxy war against India and dismantling the terrorist infrastructure in Occupied Kashmir and Pakistan. We have had fewer numbers infiltrating across the Line of Control upto the end of April 2005 but that is attributable more to the LOC fencing on the Indian side, the ceasefire and to unseasonably bad weather over the preceding three months or so. It must be noted that attempts of terrorist groups to infiltrate are continuing and a number of them have been intercepted close to the Line of Control during the period May-July and some terrorists have been killed. And as the thaw advances (May onwards) – we should expect to see more attempts to infiltrate, more contacts with our security forces and more casualties to the terrorists. The extent of support that Pakistan Army and ISI give to these terrorist groups from July onwards, will give us a clearer idea of whether the peace process has a chance of success or not.

As of now, we have to draw what comfort we can from the fact that India and Pakistan are at last talking to each other about bilateral relations across the board instead of fighting. That in itself is a significant step forward.

Before we conclude this chapter, a word about the Sri Lankan Government-LTTE talks. The problems that bedevil the relations between the Sri Lanka Government and the Tamil Tigers are many. However, they can be briefly stated as mutual hatred, distrust and total insensitivity to the Tamil's problems, on the part of the Governments of a decade or more ago. There has been a complete refusal to communicate with each other and for long periods there has been bloodshed. Nothing has been solved so far by over 20 years of fighting except, possibly, that both sides have realised that fighting will not solve anything. Therefore, the renewed talks facilitated by Norway, are most welcome and should they succeed, we may be confident that even the India-Pakistan peace process will succeed. As of now, Sri Lankan forces and LTTE are observing a ceasefire which has survived many alarms and breaches for a little over three years. If the ceasefire becomes permanent and the peace talks succeed, Sri Lanka can close a bloody chapter of internal war.

Then, truly, peace will break out all over South Asia.

Bibliography

1. Adluri Subramanyam Raju, *Terrorism in South Asia*; India Research Press, New Delhi; 2004.
2. Alvin and Heidi Toffler, *War and Antiwar*; Warner Books, New York; 1995.
3. Asghar Khan, Mohammad, *Generals in Politics.*
4. Deacon Richard, *A History of the Chinese Secret Service*; Frederick Muller Ltd, London; 1974.
5. Finer SE, *Comparative Government.*
6. Graeme Kant, *Espionage*, BT Batsford Ltd, London; 1974.
7. Henderson Harry, *Global Terrorism*; JAICO Publishing House, Mumbai; 2004.
8. HQ ARTRAC, *Indian Army Doctrine;* Shimla; October 2004.
9. Hiro Dilip, *War Without End*; Routledge, London; 2002.
10. Huntington, Samuel P, *Changing Patterns of Military Politics.*
11. Huntington, Samuel P, *The Soldier and the State.*
12. K. Cooley, *Unholy Wars*, Penguin Books, New Delhi; 2000.
13. Kahn David, *The Code Breakers*, Scriber, New York; 1996.
14. Lloyd Mark, *The Guinness Book of Espionage;* De Capo Press, Inc, New York; 1994.

15. Lt. Gen. S.L Menezes (Retd.), *Fidelity and Honour*, Oxford University Press, New Delhi; 2001.

16. Luttwak, Edward, *Coup d'etat – A Practical Handbook.*

17. Maj. Gen. R.S. Chowdhary, *A Short History of the Intelligence Corps*, Military Intelligence Training School, Pune; 1985.

18. Pamela Weintraub, *Bioterrorism*; Kensington Publishing Corporation, New York; 2002.

19. Peter Hopkirk, *The Great Game*; Oxford University Press, Oxford; 1990.

20. Philip Mason, *A Matter of Honour*, Natraj Publishers, Dehradun; 2004 (First Indian Edition).

21. Richelson Jeffry, *Sword and Shield;* Ballinger Publishing Co, USA; 1986.

22. Robert R. Glass, Col. and Philip B. Davidson, Col. *Intelligence is for Commanders*; Military Service Publishing Co, Harrisburg, Pennsylvania; 1952.

23. Rowan RW, *The Story of Secret Services*; Garden City Publishing Co, New York; 1983.

24. Stephen Philip Cohen, *The Idea of Pakistan*; Oxford University Press, New Delhi; 2004.

25. Steve Coll, *Ghost Wars*; The Penguin Press, New York; 2004.

26. Sood Sushma, *Armed Forces and Nation Building*; Arihant Publishing House, Jaipur; 1998.

27. Thapar Romila, *Ashoka and Decline of Mauryas*; Oxford University Press, New Delhi; 1973.

28. Trivedi S.D., *Secret Services in Ancient India*; Allied Publishers Private Ltd, New Delhi; 1984.

29. William R. Corson and Robert T. Crowley, *The New KGB*; William Morrow and Co, Inc, New York; 1985.

30. William V. Kennedy, Col., *The Intelligence War*, Salamander Books Ltd, London; 1983.

Index